Self-Promotion for Introverts®

The Quiet Guide to Getting Ahead

NANCY ANCOWITZ

Mc Graw Hill

New York   Chicago   San Francisco   Lisbon   London   Madrid   Mexico City
Milan   New Delhi   San Juan   Seoul   Singapore   Sydney   Toronto

7 8 9 0   QFR/QFR   1 5 4 3

ISBN   978-0-07-159129-4
MHID   0-07-159129-X

McGraw-Hill books are available at special quantity discounts to use as premiums and sales promotions, or for use in corporate training programs. To contact a representative please e-mail us at bulksales@mcgraw-hill.com.

This book is printed on acid-free paper.

Self-Promotion
for Introverts®

DEDICATED TO

you who go mum at meetings, get passed up for promotions, and would rather read about the Powers That Be than rub elbows with them. You're the brains behind the operation, the creative virtuosa, and the walking wiki. You want to make more of a difference in your life and the lives of others— but first, they need to know who you are.

Contents

Acknowledgments

This book wouldn't exist without the following people. You may find the number of them surprising, given that I'm an introvert and prefer the company of just one. I deeply value the network of friends and colleagues I've built throughout my career, and I appreciate that so many of them were there for me while I wrote this book.

The concept for this book started in 2003 as a class I created at Makor, which was at the time the West Side Center of the 92nd Street Y in New York City. I've continued to develop the class at the 92nd Street Y and the New York University (NYU) School of Continuing and Professional Studies. Special thanks go to the Makor educational director at the time, Elliott Rabin, Ph.D., for championing this idea. I'd also like to thank Howard Greenstein, Diann Witt, Dianne Mohammed, Amy Bush, and Emily Westerman who made a home for this concept at NYU. Janet Rosen, my agent at Sheree Bykofsky Associates, Inc., came to the class, helped me see the potential for this book, and shepherded it through. Thanks to Ron Idra for lending your luminous left brain for reality checks early on.

Thank you to my first editor, Lauren Lynch, for your enthusiasm and support in getting the ball rolling, and to my current incredible editor, Morgan Ertel, for the pure delight of getting to work with you. Special thanks to Jane Palmieri for your contributions as a seasoned and highly skilled EDP manager. Thank you to other members of the McGraw-Hill team whom I counted on for your expertise: Maureen Harper (production), Marci Nugent (copyediting), Staci Shands (publicity), and Heather Cooper (marketing). Special thanks to Mark Fortier at Fortier Public Relations for your fun and creative approach and PR mastery.

I am ever grateful to all of my spectacular clients, who have chosen me as their confidante and thinking partner; many of them were kind enough to share their insights on these pages. Special thanks to Bob McPeek, Ph.D., at the Center for Applications of Psychological Type, Inc. (CAPT), for generously offering your comments on my manuscript and sharing your vast knowledge and resources. Shoya Zichy, thanks for the numerous conversations and the welcome introductions, as well as for being a sounding board every step of the way. For helping me move past the mud-on-the-wall stage with editorial and research support, thank you to Andrea Galyean, Dana Leventhal, Jennifer Puk, Victoria Schwarz, and John Wilwol. Gabriella Oldham, Ed.D., and Regina Smola, thank you for outstanding administrative support.

Thanks to Carol Abrams for rooting for me the whole race and helping me realize when I had already passed the finish line, and to Steve Orr for offering grounding perspective and journalistic expertise. Jessica Seigel, thank you for your incisive insight and guidance, and thank you also to Marianna Lead, Ph.D., for illuminating the path of my journey with your brilliance. Heidi Rome, thank you for all your sharing, caring, and for speaking my language when it comes to marketing. Thanks to Dana Kaplan for listening and listening and listening to my war stories, laughing with me, egging me on, and helping me imagine this book.

Elaine Ahlberg, Bryan Chandler, Anne Fizzard, Carol Schaechter, and Ying Shiau, thanks for your ongoing friendship and moral support, which sustained me throughout this process. Karen Abrams Gerber, Ed.D., thank you for being an extraordinary source of wisdom. Thanks to Senia Maymin for your endless support and passion for research, and to Vincent Suppa, Ph.D., for being a generous colleague with an expansive mind. Special thanks to three extraordinary artists who have been an inspiration over the years: Madeline Abel-Kerns, Michael Rees, and Michael Somoroff.

For setting the gold standard for thoughtfulness, expertise, and networking savvy: Thank you to Cynthia Bemis Abrams, Analisa Balares, Michael Canterino, Ben Dattner, Ph.D., Roseanna DeMaria, Mitria Di Giacomo, John Doorley, Penny Doskow, Bob Eichinger, Janet Floyd, Bernadette Grey, Margaret A. Gomez, MCC, SPHR, Sharon Good, David Graff, Laurie Graff, Ellen Hoeppner, Annie Hoffman, Bryan Janeczko, Debra Keenan, Chris Lautenslager, PJ Lehrer, Mary Max, Caroline Adams Miller, Bob Noltenmeier, Michelle Novak, Simi Sanni Nwogugu, Gary Osland, Melissa Paller, Anthony Polanco, Dan Rubertone, Gerry Seidman, Pamela Skillings, Bobby Urband, David Vinjamuri, Troy Williams, Ruth Ann Woodley, FSA, MAAA, and Michele Wucker.

For being my dream team by reviewing all or part of my manuscript: Thank you to Brian Leahy Doyle, Annabelle Favet, Jamie Johnson at CAPT, Jonathan Goffin, Rick Lavoie, and Dan Weber.

Anne Houle, thanks for exploring every angle with me, being an outstanding sounding board, and never ceasing to make me laugh. Deep gratitude to Barbara Rubin for masterfully reading between the lines and bringing out my best and to Paul Rátz de Tagyos, another creative genius, for always going above and beyond as a friend and collaborator.

Thank you to my mother for believing I can do anything, and to my father and Ina for your unlimited encouragement and support. MJ and Rich, thanks for being an impossibly caring and bighearted sister and brother to me—not to mention my ever supportive brother-in-law Barry and sister-in-law Ellen. Isaac, thank you for your understated virtuosity, poker-faced playfulness, and deeply insightful comments, not to mention all the joy you bring me every day.

People Who Have Shared Their Wisdom in This Book

I've spoken with the following diverse array of introverts and extroverts who have generously shared their insights and tips about visibility with you.

Madeline Abel-Kerns
Opera singer, actress, and
  voice teacher

Max (Victor) Alper, Ph.D.
Fine art photographer

Lewis Bernstein, Ph.D.
Three-time Emmy Award–
  winning executive vice president
  of education and research at
  the Sesame Workshop, the
  nonprofit organization behind
  Sesame Street

Cathie Black
President of Hearst Magazines,
  a unit of Hearst Corporation,
  and author of *Basic Black*

**Michael Braunstein, ASA,
  MAAA**
Actuary; responsible for actuarial
  talent management at Aetna Inc.

Warren E. Buffett
Chairman of the board of
  Berkshire Hathaway Inc.

Susan Cain
Author of *Quiet: The Power of
  Introverts in a World That Can't
  Stop Talking* (to be published in
  2011), and president of The
  Negotiation Company

William Jefferson Clinton
Forty-second president of the
  United States

Clark Connolly*
Senior corporate training
  manager

Ben Dattner, Ph.D.
Workplace consultant and
  adjunct professor of industrial
  and organizational psychology
  at NYU

Karen Dawn
Author of *Thanking the Monkey: Rethinking the Way We Treat Animals*

Penny Doskow
President of Doskow Associates, an executive search and recruiting firm

Peter Engel
Senior recruiter at Cantor Executive Search Solutions

Doug Fidoten
President of Dentsu America, Inc., a full-service advertising and marketing- communications company

Kenneth C. Frazier
Executive vice president and president of Global Human Health, Merck & Co., Inc.

Shakti Gattegno
Educational consultant

Julie Gilbert
Founder and principal of WOLF (Women's Leadership Forum) Means Business; senior vice president of Best Buy Co., Inc., at the time of our interview

Seth Godin
Marketing guru and the author of the international bestsellers *Tribes: We Need You to Lead Us* and *Purple Cow: Transform Your Business by Being Remarkable*

Margaret A. Gomez, MCC, SPHR
Executive coach and former senior human resources leader in the advertising industry

Laurie Graff
Author-actor whose most recent book is *The Shiksa Syndrome: A Novel*

Howard Greenstein
Social media strategist and evangelist and president of the Harbrooke Group consultancy

Elizabeth Guilday
Cofounder of the Professional Certificate in Coaching program at NYU and the president of Indigo Resources Inc.

Annie Hoffman
Emmy Award–nominated broadcaster and television producer and cofounder of Sportscast Stars Training

Brad Holbrook
Actor and long-time television
    anchor

Anne Houle
Senior manager for leadership
    training at Saks Fifth Avenue

Amy Jacobs*
Technology vice president
    at a major investment bank

Debra Johnson, Ph.D.
Physiological psychologist

Earvin "Magic" Johnson
National Basketball Association
    (NBA) legend and author of *32
    Ways to Be a Champion in Business*

Gerceida Jones, Ph.D.
Master teacher of fluid dynamics
    at NYU

Francis Kelly*
Owner, consulting firm

Mac King
Comedy magician and star of the
    Mac King Comedy Magic Show
    at Harrah's in Las Vegas

Rick Lavoie
Senior account director at
    Critical Mass, a digital
    marketing agency

Marianna Lead, Ph.D.
Founder of Goal Imagery®
    Institute and former president
    of the International Coach
    Federation, New York City
    chapter

Maria Maldonado*
International banker and
    specialist in Latin American
    economic affairs

Senia Maymin
Publisher and editor in chief
    of the daily news site
    PositivePsychologyNews.com

Genevieve Menard*
Executive assistant at an
    investment bank

Bob McPeek, Ph.D.
Director of research at the Center
    for Applications of Psycho-
    logical Type, Inc. (CAPT)

Caroline Adams Miller
Author, motivational speaker,
    and professional coach

Lee E. Miller
Author with Barbara Jackson of
    *UP: Influence, Power and the
    U Perspective: The Art of Getting
    What You Want*

Charles T. Munger
Vice chairman of Berkshire
   Hathaway Inc. and chairman
   of the board and president of
   Wesco Financial Corporation

Katharine Downing Myers
Coguardian and trustee of the
   Myers-Briggs Type Indicator
   Trust

Craig Newmark
Customer service representative
   and founder of craigslist

Leonard Nimoy

Simi Sanni Nwogugu
Chief executive officer of HOD
   Consulting, Inc.

Catherine Orenstein
Founder and director of The
   OpEd Project, an initiative to
   expand public debate

Steve Orr
MarketWatch Radio Network
   anchor

Gary Osland
Account director at mNovakDesign

Ginger Parker*
Human resources executive

Michael Rees
Internationally acclaimed sculptor
   and professor of sculpture and
   digital media at William
   Paterson University

Janet Riesel, SPHR
Associate director and senior
   recruiter at Ernst & Young

Chita Rivera
Broadway legend

Heidi Rome
Marketing director at the
   UJA-Federation of New York

Harry Samuels*
Portfolio manager for a
   multi-billion-dollar
   investment portfolio

Peter Shankman
Founder of Help A Reporter
   Out (HARO)

Pamela Skillings
Author of *Escape from Corporate
   America: A Practical Guide
   to Creating the Career of
   Your Dreams*

Michael Somoroff
Award-winning artist, film
   director, and teacher

Vincent Suppa, Ph.D.
Head of the Middle Way One
World Company®, a sustainable
development organization, and
director of human resources
at a major international
European conglomerate

Jeanine Tesori
Award-winning composer of the
Broadway musicals *Caroline,
or Change* and *Thoroughly
Modern Millie*

Nicole Titus
Children's literacy advocate, artist,
and author of *Akin To No One*

Manuel Vasquez*
Operations manager at a major
nonprofit organization

David Vinjamuri
Author of *Accidental Branding:
How Ordinary People Build
Extraordinary Brands*

Kathleen Waldron, Ph.D.
President of Baruch College of the
City University of New York
(CUNY)

Pamela Wheeler
Director of operations of
the Women's National
Basketball Players
Association (WNBPA)

Lizz Winstead
Cocreator of Comedy Central's
The Daily Show and cofounder
of Air America Radio

Michele Wucker
Executive director of the
World Policy Institute,
a global think tank

Shoya Zichy
Author (with Ann Bidou) of
*Career Match: Connecting
Who You Are with What
You'll Love to Do*

The titles and organizations corresponding to each of the names above are as of
the time of each interview.

*I have changed some of my clients' names to honor their requests for confiden-
tiality.

Introduction

I've seen you silent at meetings. I've seen you eating lunch alone. And I've even seen your louder, less talented colleagues promoted over you. Yet I know you have something to say. What stops you from saying what you want to say, especially when it's about you? Perhaps you don't want to brag or draw too much attention to yourself. Compounding this, as an introvert, you prefer to think before you speak. And if you think about it long enough, some weird logic prevails about how others should figure out your strengths on their own—as if they should be able to see your merits by just looking at you. If only . . .

Wouldn't it be nice if someone would discover you? What are the chances of that happening? Considering the tough economy and job market of recent years, how long will you have to wait? If waiting just isn't an option, this book—written by an introvert for introverts—is for you. Together we'll celebrate your strengths and build the vital skills you need to raise your visibility. You'll decide how visible you need to be to accomplish what matters to you, and then you'll drive yourself toward your goals.

PROMOTING YOURSELF AUTHENTICALLY

People who are successful at gaining visibility—from Whoopi Goldberg to Donald Trump—do so in many different ways. What

Introverts and Extroverts

Introverts	Extroverts*
Get energy from "down time"	Get energy from people contact
Think before speaking or acting	Think out loud
Listen more	Talk more
Speak more softly	Speak faster and louder
Are more inclined to make deep conversation	Are more inclined to make chitchat
Prefer to speak with one or two people at a time	Prefer to work the room
Wait to be approached in social situations	Initiate conversations in social situations
Are typically reserved	Are typically active and expressive
Enjoy working alone or with one person	Enjoy working in a group
Know a lot about a few topics	Know a little about a lot of topics
Are reflective and appear more calm	Are more energetic
Are more detail oriented	Prefer faster, less complicated tasks
Need more personal space	Enjoy more people contact—the more the merrier
Are more private and hesitant about self-disclosure	Are more readily open
Have a few deep interests	Have many interests

*Also spelled "extraverts" by Carl Jung as well as the communities of the Myers-Briggs Type Indicator® (MBTI®) and other personality assessments, such as the Five-Factor Model.

Which list of attributes describes you more than 50 percent of the time—the introverts' preferences on the left or the extroverts' preferences on the right?

> **Connecting to Your Core**
>
> Self-promotion starts with self-reflection, which requires observing oneself in the lighting of awareness and without judgment. It helps to pay close attention to what you are or have rather than to emphasize what you think you're not or don't have. The more one is connected to oneself, the greater will be one's capacity to reach out. And the less one will expend energy trying to please the world.
>
> **—Shakti Gattegno, educational consultant**

works well for them may not work for you, especially if you're an introvert. Just as there is not one right way to promote yourself, there is not one right self-promotion goal. We'll find a way that works for you and helps you get wherever you want to go.

It may initially seem impossible for you to promote yourself. I encourage you to stay the course and to approach this learning with depth and intensity, which are your gifts as an introvert. Be willing to stretch as you take steps toward sharing your gifts with the world in a way that's authentic to you. You'll find your voice, create your signature presence, and speak your truth—in a big, clear voice. As Leonard Nimoy aptly shares with us: "We strive to find within ourselves our own personal voice—that which puts us in a state of grace."

GAINING VISIBILITY

Tired of no one noticing your nose glued to the grindstone? I know you produce—and you even do "double time." Who else needs to know?

Gaining visibility is a big challenge for introverts. We often immerse ourselves in our tasks, plunge the depths of our inner worlds, and neglect to come up for air to take credit for discovering New Worlds. What's an introvert to do?

Broadway legend Chita Rivera offers a piece of advice for you: "Be proud of yourself," she says. "Most of all, be proud of who you are and what you want to do. And choose your friends. Make sure you have the right energy around you, the right friendships around you. You stimulate other people and they stimulate you." That sums it up. Here's some more advice from professionals in diverse fields.

"First get clear about what you want," says Anne Houle, senior manager for leadership training at Saks Fifth Avenue. "One of the myths about promoting yourself is that you're supposed to be out there talking yourself up to everyone about everything. That's not what it's about." A client of mine we'll call Amy Jacobs, a technology vice president at a major investment bank, adds: "Think about when to use the *we* versus the *I* word. It doesn't come naturally to me because I like to give credit to my group. However, when an idea truly is mine, instead of saying *we* came up with the idea, I'm learning to say that *I* did."

"We are each an entire universe with unique value and something special to offer," says Lewis Bernstein, Ph.D., executive vice president of education and research at the Sesame Workshop, the nonprofit organization behind *Sesame Street*. "So," he adds, "like my good friend Grover on *Sesame Street* who is naturally shy, we must all find ways to let our passion and potential bubble out of us so we can share them. Sometimes that takes practice, discipline, and trial and error. It is almost always worth it." Bernstein's passion and potential have earned him and the Sesame Workshop three Emmy Awards.

QUICK TIPS TO JUMP START YOUR VISIBILITY

While we'll get into more detail later on, here are some quick tips to help you increase your visibility:

- Balance the time you spend *doing* with the time you spend *thinking* or *talking* about what you're doing.
- Take stock of what you do well by writing down your accomplishments and putting them in an "atta-girl" or

"atta-boy" file. Also include in the file congratulatory e-mails, testimonials, and glowing performance reviews you receive.

■ Practice articulating your accomplishments, and then run them by a trusted senior colleague, mentor, or coach for feedback.

■ Get on the agenda for meetings to build a platform for your ideas.

■ After meetings, write follow-up e-mails to confirm your points and contributions as well as to acknowledge those of others.

■ Stay in touch with colleagues, managers, and clients throughout your career. Let them know your comings and goings, and inquire about and celebrate theirs.

■ If you're a sociable introvert—at least, in doses—host and even speak at meetings, conferences, and social events to boost your credibility and visibility.

PROMOTING YOURSELF VERSUS OTHERS

Have you ever noticed how much easier it is to promote someone other than yourself? "There's not as much of me on the line when I try to sell you on 'Bob' than when I try to sell you on me. It's much easier to accept defeat, rejection, or ridicule on Bob's behalf than it is on mine," says actor and longtime television anchor Brad Holbrook. "Instead of worrying about coming across as arrogant or self-serving, you're advocating for someone else who deserves it," adds Heidi Rome, marketing director, UJA-Federation of New York. "Throughout my career, I've fought for the people reporting to me and won them promotions. However, when I've been up for promotions, it suddenly felt much more challenging to make the case to prove my value. Why couldn't my good work speak for itself? Now I consider it part of my job to advocate as fiercely for myself as I do for others."

"So tell me about yourself," someone says to you at a cocktail party. When you have to talk about yourself, it may feel like someone has hit the off switch on all your thoughts. So why is it not nearly as difficult to promote others? Here's why:

- It's easier to see and articulate someone else's strengths than it is your own.
- When you promote another person, you don't doubt her accomplishments the way you doubt your own.
- You take someone else's accomplishments to be a result of his talents and efforts while you take your own to be a result of dumb luck.
- You enjoy being generous with your friends by promoting them.

You may experience talking about yourself as a journey into a dusty old subterranean library of archives, getting lost in a maze of hallways, stairways, and blind turns until you crash into a wall ...in the janitor's closet. Talking about the glories of a close friend, on the other hand, may be as simple as opening a door. So since you can open that door, why not go through it too? It might take some plotting and planning. It might take plenty of practice. And it might take lots of support. The good news is that promoting yourself gets easier with practice.

EFFECTIVE SELF-PROMOTION VERSUS BRAGGING

While bragging is an obvious no-no, even quieter forms of self-promotion carry a stigma. It may seem impossible to be authentic and engaging while also promoting yourself. You're bored by other people who talk too much about themselves, and you don't want to be a bore. But if you don't talk about your accomplishments, you'll have to rely on others to do so. This can leave you feeling powerless and disappointed—not to mention invisible. While it's important for others to recognize your contributions, they first need to see your value and know what you're up to.

Let's dispel some myths about self-promotion. First, you can be a nice person and promote yourself. Next, you can promote yourself without bragging, or at the other extreme, begging. You can also do so without stretching the truth, talking someone's ear off, or pushing. You don't have to be self-centered. You also don't have to be an extrovert to do it well; instead, you can let your quiet strengths shine through and do it your way. This book is about helping you find your way.

Let's look at the differences between effective self-promotion and bragging. Simply, self-promotion at its best is articulating the overlap between what you have to offer and what your target audiences need. It enables you to solve more problems for more people

How Do You Know When People Are Saying You're a Braggart?

Circle True or False next to each of the following statements. Answer based on what you do more than 50 percent of the time.

1. I do most of the talking in social situations, and the main topic of conversation is me.　　True　　False

2. I drop names to impress people.　　True　　False

3. When I talk about myself, I just state the facts about my strengths and accomplishments.　　True　　False

4. I promote myself by matching my capabilities with my conversation partner's needs.　　True　　False

If you answered True to items 1 or 2, it's time to auction off your bullhorn on eBay. If you answered True to item 3, ask yourself if your message is relevant and interesting to your audience. If you answered True to item 4, you're on your way to effective nonbragging!

by letting them know about you. Bragging is talking *at* people, and it's all about you. It's not connected to your conversation partners—instead, it's as if they're not there. You're just talking about how outstanding you are, the phenomenal achievements you've made, and the fancy people you know. Note the glazed eyes around you. After all, isn't it tiresome when someone tries to impress you? Time to refresh your drink?

So how can you promote yourself without evacuating a room? It starts by identifying what's special about you. I can assure you there's plenty, and we'll delve into that together. Then you'll learn to speak about yourself with more confidence and tailor your message to whomever you're addressing. We'll talk about that more in Chapter 4.

A WORD ABOUT PSYCHOLOGICAL TYPES

No one on earth is exactly like you. Yet for thousands of years, scientists, philosophers, and scholars have been compelled to categorize human personalities into types—an activity called *typology*. The ancient Greeks, beginning with the physician Hippocrates, believed that our physical and mental health required an optimal balance of the four humors: blood, yellow bile, phlegm, and black bile, which corresponded with our sanguine, choleric, phlegmatic, or melancholic temperaments. (For more information, take the free Humoural Personality Test at www.passionsandtempers.com.)

Fast-forwarding a couple of millennia, one of the best studied personality assessments used today is the previously mentioned Myers-Briggs Type Indicator® (MBTI®) assessment, which was developed by Isabel Briggs Myers and her mother, Katharine Briggs, in the 1940s, and was based on the work of Swiss psychologist Carl Jung. The MBTI® tool identifies four sets, or dichotomies, of basic personality preferences. One set is extroversion (which focuses more on the outer world) and introversion (which focuses more on the inner world). The other three sets are sensing and intuition, thinking and feeling, and judging and perceiving. If you're interested in learning more about the MBTI® tool, resources abound in libraries and on the Internet; you'll find a useful starting point with myriad articles and links at www.mbtitoday.org.

Numerous other personality assessments are used, and extroversion and introversion are common to most of them. The Five-Factor Model, also referred to as the Big Five, is another major assessment. "It represents a systematic reduction from over 17,000 personality descriptors to five major factors that explain much of the ways personalities differ," notes Bob McPeek, Ph.D., director of research at the Center for Applications of Psychological Type, Inc. (CAPT). "American psychologist Gordon Allport culled these descriptors from the dictionary in the 1930s. Of these five," he adds,

Neither a Schmoozer nor a Cheerleader

As an introvert, you may feel hindered by not being a schmoozer. This starts, according to Katharine Myers, coguardian and trustee of the Myers-Briggs Trust, in the cliquey extroverted environment of the American high school, where, she says, "introverts often feel out of place because they are not inclined to hang out, chatter, make small talk, and tell jokes, which is what makes them part of a group socially. I was on the varsity team each season, a good student, editor of the paper, member of the National Honor Society, and voted girl most likely to succeed, but I felt inadequate because I did not have the skills to be what I called 'the cheerleader type.' In my senior year, I took the MBTI® and had an individual interview with Isabel Myers [who would later become Katharine Myers's mother-in-law]. I learned that there was a kind of person who preferred introversion to extroversion and that it was an okay way to be.... This information changed my life. I did not have to learn the skills of the cheerleader type. I could be myself. Now I can go comfortably into any situation anywhere in the world whether I know anyone or not."

"extroversion–introversion is arguably one of the two most important dimensions of personality." (In case you're wondering, the other "Big Two" factor is neuroticism, which is a whole other ball of wax.) Our main focus in this book is on how you can raise your visibility if you relate to being an introvert, regardless of all the other aspects of your personality—not to mention your humors!

A WORD ABOUT INTROVERSION

You may be surprised to learn that introverts comprise about half the population.[1] And, according to an article in *USA Today*, 4 in 10 top executives are introverts. In fact, the article offers Bill Gates, Warren Buffett, Charles Schwab, Steven Spielberg, and the Sara Lee Corporation chairperson and CEO Brenda Barnes as examples.[2] Add comedian Jerry Seinfeld to the list. In an interview with Oprah Winfrey, he shares that he's an introvert and adds: "I love people, but I can't talk to them. Onstage, I can."[3]

I've seen suggestions that many other high-profile people are introverts as well. However, we can never be sure unless they tell us, and not many do—possibly because of the stigma around introversion. Why can't we be sure who is actually an introvert? "There's no introvert 'gay-dar' that I can tell," says Jonathan Rauch, an opinion columnist for the *National Journal*, in an interview in *The Atlantic* magazine. The interview was inspired by a stunningly popular article that Rauch wrote titled "Caring for Your Introvert" in the March 2003 *Atlantic*. He continues: "One reason is that a lot of introverts are actually very good at being social. It just takes a lot of work for them."[4] In fact, many introverts, particularly those in highly visible roles, can be indistinguishable from extroverts, especially to the public eye. They are often in roles that require lots of people contact. Furthermore, they've often received coaching to become excellent public speakers. So it can be hard to tell who the real introverts are.

No matter. This book is for self-described introverts—and even those who just lean more toward some introverted preferences, such as having a deep conversation with one person at a time instead of working a room. You may have discovered that you were an introvert by taking a personality assessment. I took the MBTI® assessment when I was working in the corporate world and learned that I was an introvert. This helped me understand myself better and gave context to my need for quiet time—as opposed to face time—to recharge my energy and collect my thoughts. Ultimately, I reshaped my career, from being the head of a marketing team on Wall Street to being a business communication coach and speaker.

Despite the staggering bias against introversion in American society, the MBTI® tool treats extroverts and introverts as equals and doesn't place any value judgment (explicit or implicit) on one as being better than the other. "It was designed against the backdrop of the negative, 'what's wrong with you' focus evident in clinical assessments, such as the Minnesota Multiphasic Personality Inventory (MMPI) in use in the 1930s and 1940s," says Bob McPeek. The MBTI® assessment helped me see that my introversion wasn't a deficit. I became more accepting of my preference to think before I speak or act and then think again, while Jo(e) Extrovert prefers the opposite; so I became more tolerant of others.

Cathie Black, president of Hearst Magazines, shares another useful perspective: "We had a diversity course that offered much more than a narrow definition of diversity in an association I was running. The people leading the course explained the difference between extroverts and introverts: extroverts can get their energy from a roomful of people, even though [the extroverts] might be tired when they walk into that room. Introverts need time to decompress and can resurface when they've regenerated their energy." She adds: "An introvert's energy comes from being more quiet and introspective, in contrast to someone more extroverted, who accomplishes the same thing by getting energy from others." While schools of thought vary, I believe that most of us lie somewhere in the spectrum between introversion and extroversion, with fewer people at the far extremes and many of us having some characteristics of each.

SHYNESS VERSUS INTROVERSION

"Introverts are apt to be quieter, which is often interpreted as shyness," says Katharine Myers. "However, it may or may not be. Shyness has more to do with a lack of social skills. Introverts are more self-contained, which can seem shy." Notes Bob McPeek: "Though the concepts differ, introversion and shyness are often moderately correlated. In fact, introverts are more likely to be shy than extroverts, but that's not always the case."

"A lot of people confuse introversion with being shy and quiet," adds Ken Frazier, executive vice president and president of Global Human Health at the pharmaceutical giant Merck & Co., Inc. "My group at work was shocked to learn that I was an introvert." Outside of work, Frazier says, "I would just as soon read a book in my basement than engage other people, while my spouse is the life of the party. She feeds off her interactions with other people. She'll get to know everybody in the room, and I'll get to know only one or two people."

Call me a walking oxymoron: As an outgoing introvert, I look and act like an extrovert—when I'm on, that is (after sufficient quiet time). I can relate to what Jonathan Rauch shared in the *Atlantic* interview that I described earlier: "I'm not great at small talk," he says. "But I can seem quite outgoing for spells of up to an hour or so before I completely run out of gas."[5]

Introverts and extroverts alike, even those who are typically outgoing, can be shy in certain situations (e.g., among people they perceive as more powerful). Shyness can be overcome by psychotherapy and other types of self-discovery and support. Introversion, on the other hand, is not curable—and I hope you see that it's not a malady. While this book mainly addresses self-promotion for introverts as opposed to shy people of any stripe, both groups face many of the same challenges. In these pages we'll often look inward before going outward, which may be incurable too!

HIGHLY SENSITIVE PEOPLE

Many of us can benefit from the work of Elaine Aron, Ph.D., whose research-based books and other resources about highly sensitive persons (HSPs) resonate with many introverts in particular, although 30 percent of HSPs are extroverts.[6] Her Web site defines an HSP as someone whose "nervous system is more sensitive to subtleties." It adds: "Your sight, hearing, and sense of smell are not necessarily keener (although they may be). But your brain processes information and reflects on it more deeply." It also says: "Being an HSP also means, necessarily, that you are more easily overstimulated, stressed out, overwhelmed." Can you relate? You can take a self-test at www.hsperson.com to learn if you're an HSP and if you are, what you can do to make your life easier.

INTROVERTS AND EXTROVERTS: BIOLOGICAL DIFFERENCES

Are the differences between introverts and extroverts caused by biological factors in the brain— maybe even ones we're born with? Carl Jung and other major psychologists have believed this, and recent brain studies have suggested they are. These studies have been based on a variety of models, including the MBTI®; however, most of these models have categorized introverts and extroverts similarly (i.e., if you're an introvert under one model, you're likely to be one under the others). Generally, the research has found that introverts have higher levels of certain types of brain arousal and are more sensitive to some kinds of stimuli.[7]

"Introverts get more of their stimulation internally, whereas extroverts seek outside sources," says Debra L. Johnson, Ph.D., a physiological psychologist and the lead researcher on a University of Iowa study examining brain activity patterns associated with introversion and extroversion.[8] According to Johnson: "Introversion is associated with activation in areas of the brain responsible for learning, memory, planning, and language production. Extroversion is associated with areas responsible for sensory processing. Extroverts may be driven to seek sensory stimulation from other people or situations because they can't provide for their optimal level of stimulation internally." Johnson concludes: "This supports the idea that introverts tend to be more internally focused and extroverts tend to be more driven by the external environment." This makes sense to me intuitively, though I'm not a scientist. Maybe it helps explain why making chitchat with lots of people in a noisy place is difficult because it feels like there's a marching band parading inside my head. Extroverts, who are internally less stimulated, might dive into those noisy places and do a jig.

So is it better to be an introvert or an extrovert? "Rather than imagining that there is some personality profile that is uniformly good to have, let's assume that all have their strengths and pitfalls," says Daniel Nettle, Ph.D., in an article titled "The Science Behind Personality" that he wrote for the *Independent UK*. Nettle is the author of *Personality: What Makes You the Way You Are*, a book that presents increasing evidence from the work of neuroscientists, evolutionists, and geneticists on the science underlying personality type. He says in the article: "Scoring your personality won't tell you anything you don't know. It's based on how you see yourself, so logically it couldn't." He adds: "But it can reveal to you how you compare to other people, and [it] can also tap you into a wealth of accumulated psychological knowledge about the strengths and liabilities that other people similar to you have experienced."[9]

BALANCING OUR INWARD-FACING NATURE AND OUR NEED TO REACH OUTWARD

While it would be easy to portray introverts as underdogs, I'd rather underscore our advantages and foster better understanding and tolerance, regardless of personality type. "A great example of an introvert was the actress Grace Kelly, whom I met some years ago in Monte Carlo," says Shoya Zichy, author (with Ann Bidou) of *Career Match*. "She spoke at length about growing up in a family of extroverts, and how her father thought there was something wrong with her because all she wanted was to go to her room and read. Then she became an actress, got rich and famous, and finally won her battle that way. As an actress," Zichy says, "she got to play other people. And the lines were already made up for her."

While the inward-facing nature of introverts can be a source of strength, if we neglect to reach outward, we miss out on the richness that human interaction can bring—not to mention the career advancement associated with our increased visibility. Kelly found an elegant balance between going inward and outward—and all the world got to benefit.

WHY I WROTE THIS BOOK

This book enables me to share my experiences and help as many people as possible—particularly introverts—to promote themselves more adeptly. I've spoken with insightful introverts and extroverts from all walks of life, not to mention a few giants like Cathie Black (Hearst Magazines); Warren Buffett; President Bill Clinton; marketing guru Seth Godin; Earvin "Magic" Johnson; Katharine Myers (Myers-Briggs Trust); Craig Newmark (founder of craigslist); Leonard Nimoy; and Chita Rivera. See what you can learn about visibility from their collective wisdom.

My perspective integrates the various lenses through which I see the world: as a businessperson, a communication coach, and an artist. I draw from more than two decades' experience as both an entrepreneur and a corporate marketing vice president as well as my after-hours life as a playwright. I've been keeping copious notes from the trenches, from selling my wares to major retailers and getting national press as a young jewelry designer to getting credit for my accomplishments and learning how to be heard at meetings at major financial firms on Wall Street.

While you may be interested in the robust body of psychological literature exploring the world of introversion, this book is by and for laypeople. The main focus of the book is raising your visibility in your professional life as an introvert. However, what you'll learn can also be helpful in your personal life. Skills such as networking are useful in both.

My intention is to offer a place for you to explore and a springboard for you to be heard and seen by the people and organizations you want to impact. I want you to get more credit for your ideas, become more visible wherever you want to be noticed, earn more money if that's your goal, and ultimately make greater contributions to society.

First we'll go inward, which is most likely within your comfort zone as an introvert, and then we'll go outward. We'll cover everything from mitigating the self-doubt and negativity inside your head to identifying what's special about you; from making a game plan to getting into action mode. You can read this book cover to cover, skip around, or skim. I welcome you to proceed at a pace that stimulates yet doesn't overwhelm you.

In Chapter 1 we'll go eyeball-to-eyeball with those demons inside you who cheer on the sidelines every time you misspeak or misstep—or prevent you from stepping out much at all. They whisper nasty reminders of all your faults and weaknesses. Of course, they would have you believe that you can't live without them. Can you relate? Yet how can you promote yourself when the voices in your head are constantly reminding you of all your shortcomings? How convincing can you be at selling yourself if you're not convinced of your own value? We'll go inward to take stock of your strengths, talk back to those sniping voices, and emerge stronger and ready to go after what's important to you.

Ready to go inward, outward, and onward?

one

Your Negative Self-Talk

Tuning Out U–SUCK Radio

It's a good thing that we can't hear each other think. People only pick up on what you give off—verbally and nonverbally. So before you promote yourself outwardly, let's take a look at how you talk to yourself inwardly. Are the messages you say to yourself gentle and forgiving, petty and ruthless, or somewhere in between? What if your accomplishments weren't just an accident? And what if you're actually gifted—rather than just pretending or duping lots of people?

In this chapter we'll discuss what you can do to mitigate your negative chatter. We'll also address its overbearing companion: the need to make everything perfect—the first time, no excuses. Not that introverts have cornered the market for negative self-talk and its close cousin, perfectionism. We'll discuss what you can do to redirect this self-defeating energy.

Being able to overcome one's insecurities is the prerequisite to understanding how one can serve others and take meaningful actions in the world, which result in greater community, and is predicated on our ability to come outside ourselves and share with others.

—Michael Somoroff, award-winning artist, film director, and teacher

I'll provide you with specific examples and simple tools. You'll take stock of your own negative self-talk, better manage your self-directed put-downs, and build an inner circle of support. While some of the examples I'll share are bleak, I'll also refer to the victories of two world-class swimmers for inspiration. All of this is to illustrate that the challenge of negative self-talk is a big, yet surmountable, one; it's also universal. Why are we even addressing negative self-talk? The better you manage it, the more you can bring out your most confident, supremely promotable introverted self to ultimately make greater contributions to society.

INTROVERTS MAY ACTUALLY CHATTER MORE—IN THEIR HEADS

Research on the brain suggests that introverts may have a higher level of internal chatter than extroverts. Debra L. Johnson, Ph.D., a physiological psychologist, recommends that introverts embrace their inner dialog. "If the dominant functional pattern is to engage in a running monolog about activities and demands, this self-talk might be harnessed by explicitly 'reminding' oneself about important behaviors," she says. "For example, a person might include a self-comment to the effect of, 'I did really good work on that project—everyone has told me that.' Or 'In a staff meeting today, I have to speak up about my involvement.' Or he or she could even plan and rehearse exactly what to say in a meeting."[1]

Bob McPeek, Ph.D., director of research at the Center for Applications of Psychological Type, Inc. (CAPT), adds: "If you look across different areas of research, there is a pattern of evidence suggesting that introverts are more likely to engage in self-reflection. Much of it is along the lines of tossing and turning at 3 a.m., replaying the same event in your mind, and beating yourself up for it," he says. Can you relate? McPeek continues: "Different researchers use words like 'brooding' or 'rumination' for this negative state. An effective strategy for dealing with it is distracting yourself or diverting your energy. There's also a positive side to self-reflection that introverts may exhibit that is more like a healthy intellectual curiosity about yourself." We entertain that curiosity throughout this book.

A CHALLENGE WORTH TAKING ON

Like maintaining an exercise program or keeping your finances in order, managing your negative self-talk is a challenge worth taking on. At the Self-Promotion for Introverts® workshops I offer for adults at New York University, most of my students—who include entrepreneurs, architects, psychotherapists, artists, computer programmers, investment bankers, Harvard-educated lawyers, marketing executives, corporate managers, and nonprofit directors—anonymously share their negative self-talk messages on index cards. I collect the cards and read them to the room. Here's what these accomplished professionals have shared:

- ▪ "I'll never make decent money doing anything I like."
- ▪ "My biggest accomplishments were all flukes."
- ▪ "I'm a failure."
- ▪ "I'm always the invisible 'brains' behind the operation."
- ▪ "As soon as an idea comes out of my mouth, someone else takes credit."
- ▪ "My mind goes blank when I try to converse with new people."
- ▪ "I sound stupid."
- ▪ "I'll spend the rest of my life as a worker bee."
- ▪ "I appear mentally slow because I need to collect my thoughts before I speak."
- ▪ "There's something wrong with me for being so private."

Recognize these? Do they sound familiar? Thoughts like these may stream through your head too—perhaps at four in the morning, when your tongue goes bone dry at the podium, or when your boss storms into your cubicle demanding a summary of your whole year's accomplishments. How are you supposed to promote yourself while those menacing flying monkeys from *The Wizard of Oz* are screeching insults inside your head?

INVISIBLE, YET ALL EYES ARE ON YOU

Let's say you're an award-winning graphic designer with a solid core of Fortune 500 clients. However, when you enter a holiday party full of highly accomplished senior managers, many of whom are potential clients, you find yourself frequently looking out the window, checking your voice mail, and visiting the restroom. What's keeping you from cracking a smile and striking up a conversation? Maybe something like the following is running through your head: "Everyone here is more accomplished, better educated, more informed, and more interesting than I am."

After deliberating for two hours, you finally get up the courage to approach someone. You say something to the nearest person in a raspy mumble without making eye contact. The potential client of a lifetime interrupts your first (and only!) sentence and quickly takes off, waving vaguely at someone across the room. You slink away and go home, ironically feeling that all eyes were on you and your major social faux pas—despite your invisibility. To make matters worse, you mockingly replay in your head your opening line to the potential client extraordinaire: "How's the sangria?" It takes three months before you're ready to consider your next outing.

HOW TO MAKE NETWORKING SITUATIONS MORE PALATABLE

It doesn't have to be like this. In Chapter 5 we'll discuss more about the external aspects of navigating networking situations. Meanwhile, here are a few quick tips you can use right away:

- **Choose events where you're likely to feel welcome.**
- Before going to a networking event, **take stock of why someone would want to talk to you.**
- **Do something that makes you feel grounded** just before the event (e.g., write, draw, listen to a favorite song, or call a mentor).
- **Scope out the most comfortable places**—possibly the quietest areas—for you in the space (just not the wall!).
- **Remember that all eyes aren't on you.**
- **Learn about other people**—listen intently, solve their problems, and share resources.
- **Remember to breathe.** We often forget this most basic human need. Taking a few deep breaths will help you relax.
- **Drink water.** Stay hydrated for your overall well-being and specifically for your voice. Avoid caffeinated beverages, which can contribute to the jitters.

YOU CAN CATCH ANY BALL

One of my clients, a senior corporate training manager—let's call him Clark Connolly—found a way to stay attuned to his gifts, despite the background "noise." He shares a recurring negative self-talk message that plays in his head when he speaks to someone more senior: "I'm not in the same league." To counter that, I ask Connolly to describe a situation in which he performs at his best. A fine and confident athlete, he pictures himself in the outfield and says, "I can catch any ball." Connolly repeats this affirmation to himself whenever he faces a particularly challenging situation; in fact, it's become his mantra.

While we'll talk more about affirmations in the next chapter on strengths, you might start thinking of a positive message that you can say to yourself. Connolly wrote his affirmation, along with other useful reminders, on a little card and laminated it. He refers to this wallet card whenever he needs a boost, like before a high-stakes meeting. Here's what it says:

Clark Connolly's Negative Self-Talk Antidote Wallet Card

- **Preparation.** Anticipate.
- **Breathing.** Ten deep breaths.
- **Affirmations.** "I can catch any ball."
- **Physical attributes.** Feet planted; head high; shoulders back.
- **Voice.** Modulate; lower pitch; raise volume; ask questions; show interest.

While referring to your own version of Clark Connolly's wallet card may recharge you with positive thoughts, it can also help you manage those nasty little nothings that murmur between your ears. I find that managing my negative self-talk requires daily maintenance, especially when I'm under a lot of stress. During those times, I attempt to be more conscious of the messages I say to myself. I counter the noise by reinforcing what I'm good at, putting myself in positive situations, and surrounding myself with people who believe in me. I encourage you to find what works best for you.

PERFECTIONISM

A challenge that some of us face that can go hand-in-hand with negative self-talk is our unending quest to make everything perfect. Consider this: You interview for a high-paid position at a prestigious law firm. Your credentials and background are an ideal match for the position and the firm. You meet with three partners in a series of interviews and give excellent answers, despite four hours of relentless grilling. However, you make one mistake. While you're saying good-bye to the senior partner on your last interview, you accidentally launch a minuscule projectile of saliva, which lands on her cheek. While the partner doesn't seem to notice and you appear calm, later, when thinking about the interviews, you're convinced you bombed. Why? All you can think about is that you spat at the senior partner. So your perfectionism fuels your negative self-talk, which says: "I'm a total idiot for spitting. I blew it and can't get anything right." You picture what went wrong—over and over, in a slow-motion playback of the trajectory of spittle—and you ignore the overwhelming majority of things that went right.

Chita Rivera offers some gentle wisdom and a grounded perspective that might help you counter the dual demons of perfectionism and negative self-talk: "Enjoy what you do—even the things that seem negative," she says. "Know that they're lessons. Everything is a lesson." She adds important reminders that you've probably heard but are so easy to forget: "Don't take yourself too seriously, and have a sense of humor."

To give you a personal example of how I've managed my perfectionism and negative self-talk, I'll share what it was like writing this book. Confession: I find writing to be at times excruciating. It's a form of self-expression that brings out all my demons. I picture those flying monkeys tangled up in my every word. If my writing doesn't meet my standards on the first draft (which never happens), the monkeys scream and hiss at me, and my natural inclination is to stop writing—or to not even start.

I refused to succumb this time. So first, I asked myself: What do I want to achieve? Answer: To write a book to help introverts advance in their careers. Next, I asked myself: What resources do I have to achieve my goal? Answer: I've compiled tips and techniques from the trenches as an entrepreneur and corporate vice president who is an introvert. And most recently, as a business communication coach and lecturer, I've helped countless introverts thrive in an extroverts' world. Lastly, I asked: What has been my biggest obstacle? Answer: My fears. Specifically, the negative self-talk that can stymie me, keeping me from even taking the first step. Not to mention the peril, the tyranny, of perfectionism.

The Pros and Cons of Perfectionism

While I'm not a perfectionist, I've worked around them my entire career, and all the entrepreneurs I interviewed in my book were perfectionists. In a way perfectionists have an advantage because they can correct small things that customers will perceive and most marketers won't notice. Of course, an 80 percent solution that you implement is better than a 100 percent solution that never happens. If you take small steps, even if they're not perfect, they'll do more for your business than if you try to create perfect programs to put in the marketplace. The trick is that you can't let perfectionism paralyze you.

—**David Vinjamuri, author of** *Accidental Branding:*
How Ordinary People Build Extraordinary Brands

Can you relate to being so scared that you can't even write or say your first word or take your first step toward something important to you? Simi Sanni Nwogugu, CEO of HOD Consulting, Inc., a diversity consulting organization, shares some fitting advice: "Get out of your head once in a while and do an activity that's fun and refreshing. Then return to the task at hand with new energy. Sometimes the best insights occur when we're not concentrating so hard."

YOUR STALWARTS

Most of us can benefit from outside support to help us reach our goals. Take stock of who is most likely to celebrate your successes. Jot down a list of these champions, including friends, family members, colleagues, mentors, acquaintances from your volunteer work, and former bosses, that make up your dream team. (I like the term, which is also a nod to the U.S. basketball team that won the gold medal at the Olympics in 1992, thanks in large part to such greats as Michael Jordan, Larry Bird, and Earvin "Magic" Johnson, who offers advice for you in the next chapter.) Include people on your dream team with whom you could build relationships—either by deepening existing ones or by starting new ones.

YOUR DREAM TEAM

List the names of current and prospective members of your dream team in the far-left column in the table that follows. Then put a check mark in the boxes to the right that correspond to the types of support that each person can offer you. You can check multiple boxes for each person.

Now that you've identified your dream team, I have a highly rewarding exercise for you, which is similar to one described in a 2005 article titled "How to Play to Your Strengths" in the *Harvard Business Review*.[2] Quite a few of my coaching clients have reaped the benefits of this exercise, which has underscored their strengths and added to their base of support. Here's the drill:

1. Pick three to five people from your dream team and ask them if they would take 10 to 15 minutes to help you with your visibility efforts—and ultimately your personal and career development.
2. Ask those who agree to e-mail you three things that they appreciate most about you—including your personality traits, talents, accomplishments, and good deeds. We're not looking for anything critical of you in this list—strictly the positive. If you're more comfortable receiving their feedback anonymously, you could follow the advice of Diane Darling, author of *The Networking Survival Guide*, to use an online tool such as SurveyMonkey.com.[3]

Current Dream Team

Contact's Name	Confidante	Advisor	Mentor	Cheerleader	Other (Specify)

Prospective Additions to Your Dream Team

Contact's Name	Confidante	Advisor	Mentor	Cheerleader	Other (Specify)

3. Review their comments and reflect on the attributes they see in you that you may take for granted.
4. Print out the input you receive and keep it at hand.

Some clients who have done this exercise talk about how uplifting it is to refer to these reinforcements from their dream team. It not only feels good but it also helps create a strong foundation for your visibility efforts. Take a moment to consider the positive impact you've had on the people who matter to you. What is it like for you to receive this concrete evidence, in writing, of just how capable and talented you are?

Refute Negative Self-Talk instead of Compliments

How do you respond to compliments? Do you deflect them or say that you don't really deserve them? You may be so used to minimizing compliments that you're not even aware that you're doing it. By denying a compliment, you are not only putting yourself down but you're also slighting the person who offered it by doubting her judgment or suggesting that her standards aren't high. Instead, why not graciously say, "Thank you"?

YOUR NAYSAYERS

Just as praise can give you a boost, criticism can drain your energy and distract you from your attempts to raise your visibility. Have you ever had a friend whom you could always count on to remind you of your weaknesses, minimize your accomplishments, or put you down? As if your negative self-talk weren't enough to contend with. "I've had friends like that, but I can't afford to be around them," says my client Madeline Abel-Kerns, opera singer, actress, and voice teacher. "I've also had vocal coaches and mentors like that, but I prefer the ones that give praise and encouragement, which is the approach I take with my students; otherwise, the learning process is much too harsh. In my early and middle development," she reflects, "I was negative toward myself, so I just accepted negativity in my mentors. Now I won't put up with it. I work hard to encourage myself and expect it from others."

While you can't control what other people say to you, you may be able to control whom you spend time with. Why waste your energy by exposing yourself to additional noise? Here are a couple of criteria to help you identify your naysayers:

1. When you talk about your victories, they typically change the subject to theirs, compare yours unfavorably to others', minimize your accomplishments, or "one-up" you.
2. They put you down. Some people will tell you that they're just being brutally honest, even if you don't want to hear it or if the timing is off for you. Feedback is most effective when you agree to receive it.

"If you were to look deeper into the choices your naysayers made in their lives, there's a good chance that they had a hope or dream they decided not to go for," says Lizz Winstead, cocreator of *The Daily Show* and cofounder of Air America Radio. "So when you stand before them, willing to put yourself out there to make the world a better place or make yourself a better person, there's a pain inside them. They're telling you not to pursue your dreams because they don't want to see you succeed where they didn't take a chance."

NOT BUYING IN TO YOUR DETRACTORS

"I worked for a radio network where I wasn't on the air," says Steve Orr, MarketWatch Radio Network anchor. "It was the most miserable period of my career. They treated me like a factory part. I went to the guy in charge and gave him my demo tape, and he told me point-blank: 'We have a certain bar here, and you just don't meet it.'"

Orr describes what he did about it: "I could have reacted two different ways. I could either think, 'Oh, my God, I really suck. He doesn't like the way I sound. He doesn't like my style. I'm no good.' But instead, I took it as a huge challenge that motivated me to get out of there and get back on the air. And now I'm at a much better place, making double the money, and on far better stations. So just because someone else doesn't believe in you doesn't mean that you should lose faith in yourself." Orr adds: "I shored up the confidence to achieve my goal. I would not let them beat me."

What can you do about your naysayers? You may feel bad after interacting with them. They don't believe in you, don't really "get" you, and may be competitive with you or jealous. Yet you continue to maintain contact with them out of habit or out of concern that you would offend them or cause a stir in your mutual circle of friends if you were to distance yourself. However, do you really need someone to remind you of your missteps? So whom, if anyone, do you need to distance yourself from? Abel-Kerns shares an upbeat insight: "The more I've worked at being positive, the more positive energy is in my life."

U-SUCK

You hear an inescapable Fran Drescher voice from the hit 1990s CBS sitcom *The Nanny* grating in your head. It's a big chatterbox, an endless broadcast with the call letters U-SUCK—AM, FM, and satellite too. You can't seem to change the dial. It's as if you're stuck in the dentist's chair with your mouth wide open and your ears glued to headphones that are blaring every half-truth of the popular U-SUCK rhetoric into your captive brain: "You're a loser . . . you're behind where you should be for your age . . . you're a fraud . . . you're boring!"

Haven't you heard enough U-SUCK? You could let it rule, or you could turn it down, tune it out, and change the dial to a station sponsored by your dream team, which plays a completely different tune, with lyrics such as "You're incredibly gifted with language." Or "You're observant and have a keen eye for detail."

TALK BACK, SHOUT OUT

It helps to create a strong arsenal of responses to our negative self-talk. In the column on the left in the table that follows, write three of the most common negative messages you say to yourself. In the column on the right, write your rebuttals—or, at the very least, responses. Make your refutations based on fact and on what your most ardent dream team member would say. If you need help with this, why not ask her or him?

Your Negative Self-Talk	Your Refutations
Example: I'm incapable of speaking to anyone important.	*Example: Nonsense. I'm important myself, and here's why: As a strategic thinker, I excel at crisis management and have helped major organizations rebound from even the most serious public relations disasters.*
1.	1.
2.	2.
3.	3.

TUNE IN TO U-ROCK

Even if you don't hear it anywhere else on a given day, you can always rely on U-ROCK to sing your praises. So if U-SUCK is playing its usual programming, which is geared to put you in your place 24/7, don't forget that you can always choose to tune in to U-ROCK instead.

In the space that follows, write three of your strengths and accomplishments that differentiate you; they can be from any aspect of your life. Be as specific and concrete as possible. Refer to the reinforcements your dream team shared with you for a jump start.

My strengths

1. _____

_____

2. _____

_____

3. _____

_____

My accomplishments

1. _____

_____

2. _____

_____

3. _____

_____

WHAT YOU FOCUS ON GROWS

In this chapter I hope you've become more aware of the negative tape loop that plays inside your head. "Even if you think that its messages have some truth to them, you can still thank them for sharing and choose to focus elsewhere," says Anne Houle, a senior manager for leadership training at Saks Fifth Avenue who is also trained in counseling psychology.

In wrapping up, I'd like to share an anecdote that illustrates one of my favorite concepts, which may already be familiar to you: what you focus on grows. I read a story in the *New York Times* by polar explorer and environmentalist Lewis Gordon Pugh, who talks about his experience of diving into a glacial lake in Norway to vie for the world record for the longest swim in ice water. One expert said a normal person attempting such a feat would have been disabled within seconds and dead within two or three minutes.

Just before Pugh dived in, his mind coach gave him a pep talk, reminding him that he had pioneered more swims than anyone else in history, was the only person who had swum in all five oceans of the world, and was the only person to have swum in the Arctic and Antarctic oceans.

Pugh plunged into the icy waters. Children were waving Norwegian flags and cheering "Heia Lewis! Heia!" (Go Lewis! Go!). Finally, despite massive hyperventilation and being frozen and exhausted, Pugh had set a world record for the longest swim in ice water: 1,200 meters in 23 minutes and 50 seconds.[4] Imagine what would have happened if instead Pugh's coach had said: "Lewis, you're looking awfully bloated. Are you sure you're up for this today? You should have listened to your mother and become an accountant. I'll be waiting for you in the life-support boat. Good luck. Ready, set, heia!" The starting gun is fired, and what do you think happens now? Again, what you focus on grows.

Another great swimmer, Michael Phelps, comes to mind when I think of the mantra "what you focus on grows." The most decorated Olympiad of all time, Phelps was a mediocre student with attention deficit hyperactivity disorder (ADHD).[5] One of Phelps's teachers told his mother, "Your son will never be able to focus on anything." Still, he conquered his childhood fear of being underwater only to discover that he was really a big fish who loved more than anything to swim past all the other fish.[6] With the support of his family and his coach, he refused to listen to the chorus of couldn'ts—and instead focused on soaring through water, all the way to Beijing. I never tire of *The Little Engine That Could* types of stories. How can this play out in your life?

Now that we've talked about how to prevent your negative self-talk from stymieing your visibility, we'll turn our discussion to more about what's amazing about you. In the next chapter we'll talk about how to further identify and articulate your strengths. After all, if you can't do it, who else can?

REFLECTIONS AND ACTIONS

Before we move on, take a moment to gather your thoughts and insights, take stock of what you learned in this chapter, and jot down how you can apply the learning. We'll do this at the end of each chapter, and by the end of the book you'll have created a learning journal along with concrete plans. I also recommend seeking out the support that you'll need to accomplish these plans. This can entail sharing with a friend, mentor, or coach; it can also entail forming a community by blogging or joining an online group.

What you learned

1. _____

_____

_____

2. _____

_____

_____

3. _____

_____

_____

Action: What will you do?	How You'll Do It: What support or further information will you obtain?	Accountability: Whom will you tell about this action?	Completion Date: By when?

two

Your Strengths

Tuning In U–ROCK Radio

Why is it important to see your own strengths? Because if you can't see them, how are you supposed to shape your personal brand or define what sets you apart from the rest of the crowd? Of course, you can promote yourself more generically just like any other accountant who's good with numbers, academic who reads lots of research, or illustrator with a flare for color. Or you can mine your rich inner world and get a little more creative when calling out your strengths.

Imagine driving along the NJ-495 roadway, which dramatically scoops around and dips down the cliffs of Weehawken, New Jersey, into a huge industrial no-man's-land before you enter the Lincoln Tunnel to the legendary city of Broadway, big business, and billionaire dreams. As you navigate your way through this sea of gray, peppered with smokestacks and billboards, your eyes jump from ads for SmartWater to iPhones to one about you.

Now imagine what your billboard would say, how it would look, and what image it would convey. How does your introverted self want to be seen by the outside world? Which of your magnificent qualities could you display? How can you summarize your offerings in a snapshot that will grab drivers going 60 miles per hour and hold the attention of commuters stuck in traffic as well?

There's no room for lots of words or complicated images. And there's no room for anything that's less than sparkling about you. At the end of this chapter you'll design your own billboard. Meanwhile, we'll go on a journey to help you determine the message and image you'd like to project. While, of course, I'm not suggesting that you actually buy a billboard ad (although it might be a novel approach), this mental excursion will remind you to make your message quick and clear—or else you'll pay more than the toll!

As you go through this chapter think of your strengths as gems that we'll look at from different angles. In Chapter 1 we lassoed your negative self-talk. After shushing, rebutting, or even just acknowledging the flying monkeys between your ears, you identified three of your strengths and three of your accomplishments. Use these as a foundation for the work we'll do in this chapter. We'll explore more about your strengths, particularly the ones that are unique to you. Then we'll talk about how you can use those strengths to get more grounded, or more confident. Lastly, we'll explore how to promote yourself authentically. We'll zoom in on what you've got, rather than on what you're missing. Again, what you focus on grows.

We're about to celebrate you. This may sound too fluffy for someone of your intellect. However, there's empirical evidence for the benefits of cheering yourself on. "Since the birth of the positive psychology movement a decade ago," says Caroline Adams Miller, an author, motivational speaker, and professional coach, "research has proven that certain 'interventions' into one's behavior can enhance one's well-being. One of the most potent interventions is focusing on one's unique talents."

Miller continues: "Chris Peterson, a professor of psychology at the University of Michigan, and Martin Seligman, the 'father of positive psychology,' created the well-validated Signature Strengths test—also called the VIA (Values in Action). Their studies have shown that people who focus on their top five 'signature strengths,' which can be determined by taking their free

Web-based survey,[1] are happier than people who don't." Here's how Miller explains it: "This is because when we lead with our strengths instead of our weaknesses, we come across as more authentic, we put people at ease, and have more energy." She adds: "Also, the Gallup Organization found that discovering an employee's top strengths and tailoring his or her job description to take advantage of those strengths leads to happier and more productive employees and work teams." According to *Strengths Finder 2.0* by Tom Rath, which builds on a vast body of research by scientists at Gallup: "Our studies indicate that people who *do*

Magic Strengths

My boyfriend Isaac and I waited in a long, snaking line at a book signing for Earvin "Magic" Johnson's *32 Ways to Be a Champion in Business* at a Barnes & Noble near New York's Grand Central Station. In the chapter titled "Focus on Strengths," Johnson talks about his fellow basketball legend Michael Jordan's failed baseball career and his own short-lived stint as a late-night talk-show host for *The Magic Show.* Johnson shares how he and Jordan both made the mistake of trying to capitalize on their weaknesses instead of sticking with their strengths. He ends the chapter by saying: "I've already proved I'll never be Leno or Arsenio. No matter how hard I might try, I'll never be Warren Buffett or Bill Gates either. Yet I have been able to attain my own brand of business success by focusing on my knowledge and credibility in urban markets..."[3]

The woman standing in line in front of me, a lifelong fan of Johnson's, tells me she got special permission from her boss to duck out of work to be there. When it's her turn, Johnson gives her his undivided attention amid the chatter of fans, handlers, and security detail. They hug. He signs. I'm next. Conscious of the line, we exchange niceties, he flashes his celebrated smile, and I toss him the ball: In one biggish sound bite, I tell Johnson I'm writing this book and ask his advice for my readers.

"First of all, know yourself and believe in yourself," he says. "If you know yourself, you will know your strengths and weaknesses. You will play to your strengths and try to enhance your weaknesses. Then understand the climate of the workplace: Who are really the decision makers? What do they like and what don't they like? What do they want to see in their employees?" Then, he says with emphasis: "Overdeliver."

One of Johnson's strengths is immediately apparent. Johnson and I talked for only a minute; however, he created the feeling as if it was just the two of us chatting over coffee. He gets three points for presence! I imagine his days as the king of no-look passes, doing his precision dance amid the uproar of an action-packed court. Today, as a successful entrepreneur and community leader, he still tunes out the noise and keeps his eye on the ball. That quality of concentration is something many of us introverts excel at. It helps us build deep one-on-one relationships and gain detailed knowledge.

have the opportunity to focus on their strengths every day are *six times as likely to be engaged in their jobs* and more than *three times as likely to report having an excellent quality of life in general.*"[2] Not a bad argument for focusing on our strengths! Furthermore, until you can actually embrace what's special and different about you, it's going to be a hard sell trying to get anyone else to do so.

INTROVERSION AS A STRENGTH

In a society in which we're expected to dazzle and be dazzled, from pitching venture capitalists by day to rubbing against high-powered elbows at night, introverts are often thought of as outcasts who quietly lurk in the margins. If you subscribe to that stigma, why not cancel your subscription? Instead, focus on your introverted strengths. Since you spend more time listening than talking, you can process what you learn to target your audiences effectively. "Quieter people should recognize that they have an advantage: When they speak, it's usually in more measured, thoughtful tones," says Ken Frazier, executive vice president and president of Global Human Health at Merck & Co., Inc. "I think it's an advantage to speak comparatively rarely, but clearly and forcefully. Introverts can make up for quantity with quality."

PROSPECTING FOR YOUR STRENGTHS

For introverts in particular, promoting yourself is first about thinking, then about taking action, and lastly about reflecting on our actions. As an introvert you're well suited to prospect for your inner gems, mine them, and refine them for the outside world. The clearer we are about our offerings, the stronger we are at promoting ourselves. "Examine those offerings," says Margaret A. Gomez, MCC, SPHR, executive coach and former senior human resources leader in the advertising industry. "They're yours," she notes. "They're about the value you have, the impact you make, and the distinction you bring. No one else can replicate that. The DNA is yours."

YOUR INTROVERTED STRENGTHS

Ready to do a little digging? Let's start by looking at activities introverts excel at that we often prefer to do either alone or possibly with one other person. On a scale of 1 to 5, with 1 being very weak and 5 being very strong, rate your abilities at each of the following:

_____   Researching

_____   Concentrating

_____   Gaining expertise

_____ Thinking things through before you speak or act

_____ Writing

_____ Working independently

_____ Building deep, lasting relationships

_____ Listening attentively

What insights have you had by assessing your introverted strengths? Which of these strengths can you rely upon most to help you raise your visibility?

_____

_____

What other strengths (e.g., persistence, trustworthiness, creativity, technical ability) do you have that can help you achieve that visibility?

_____

_____

MINING YOUR GEMS

We're so used to our own strengths that many of us take them for granted. We also tend to focus on our tangible headline accomplishments (or lack thereof!) rather than on paying attention to which of our strengths are most important to our clients, managers, and other target audiences.

Let's look inward again and answer the following questions to discover more about your strengths and accomplishments. As an aside, you really know you're an introvert if you're willing to do these exercises! Why? While your extroverted colleagues are busy extroverting, you're more likely to spend time collecting and analyzing data, reflecting, and even quietly strategizing.

1. What is the one thing you've accomplished that you're most proud of? Which of your strengths came into play?

   _____

   _____

2. Briefly describe a time when you solved a problem that made someone's life easier. Name three of the strengths you used to solve the problem.

   _____

   _____

3. What is the last thing you did that someone appreciated? (Your answer doesn't have to be work related.)

   _____

   _____

4. If your most stalwart supporter were asked the three things she or he likes best about you, what would they be?

   _____

   _____

5. Whom do you admire? Which qualities do you admire most about her or him?

   _____

   _____

Reflect on your answers to these questions. What insights come to mind?

DIGGING DEEPER: DISCOVERING MORE ABOUT YOUR GEMS

Use the strengths you just identified as a starting point for the exercise you're about to do. This will help you delve deeper into what's really special and different about you, what hinders you, and what brings out your strengths. While identifying your strengths may feel like a far cry from the concrete work of raising your visibility and making more money (or whatever your self-promotion goals are), it is at the core of successfully promoting yourself.

When you list your strengths and write what makes them different or special in the table that follows, I encourage you to be as specific as possible. While this book is mainly focused on business, in this exercise I recommend that you jot down anything that's positive about you that comes to mind, regardless of what it's connected to, be it your career or personal life, your introversion, or other aspects of your personality. For example, some of my clients have shared that their strengths include powerful problem-solving abilities, strong intuition, and an acute ability to see the big picture while keeping track of all the details. If you have a hard time filling in the "What makes your strengths different and/or special?" column, ask for assistance from a member of your dream team, which you assembled in Chapter 1.

For the column titled "What inhibits your strengths?" think of all the things that annoy, undermine, minimize, intimidate, and frustrate you. For example, in my case, when I'm exposed to excessive noise, crowds, bad smells, and too much visual stimulation, my introverted self becomes turtlelike and retreats into a protective shell.

In the far-right column titled "What brings out your strengths?" think of the internal and external factors that encourage you to flourish. Introverted clients have written in activities like seeking out a quiet environment, drinking a soothing beverage, listening to a favorite song, speaking with a mentor, and taking a nap. In the first row of the table, opera singer Madeline Abel-Kerns shares one of her responses to help get you started.

Your Strengths: List your top 5 strengths below. Circle your introverted strengths.	What Makes Your Strengths Different and/or Special?	What Inhibits Your Strengths?	What Brings Out Your Strengths?
Example from Madeline Abel-Kerns: Charisma	*My ability to connect with people in an honest way, without artifice. I think I'm that way one-on-one and when I perform.*	*When I worry how others will perceive me.*	*When I trust myself.*
1.			
2.			
3.			
4.			
5.			

So much has been written in recent years in the burgeoning field of positive psychology about the importance of identifying our strengths. Books and articles by Martin Seligman, Ph.D., Tal Ben-Shahar, Ph.D., Tom Rath, Marcus Buckingham, and the late founder of the strengths psychology movement, Donald Clifton, Ph.D.—not to mention recent additions by Sonja Lyubomirsky, Ph.D., Caroline Adams Miller, Senia Maymin, and Margaret Greenberg—are accessible to laypeople and can help you further explore this important concept.

"As complex beings, we all have lots of strengths and resources," says Michael Rees, a professor of sculpture and digital media at William Paterson University and an internationally acclaimed sculptor. "Different situations call for different strengths. Allow yourself to be wherever you are, so you can't be ahead or behind—don't berate yourself for not being where you think you should be." Rees compares strengths to muscles, which have to be continually exercised to thrive.

Now that we've started to unearth your strengths, how can we reinforce them?

HOW TO GET GROUNDED (OR BUILD YOUR CONFIDENCE)

When I think about being grounded, I picture a grand old oak tree with its roots planted deep into the earth. The oak tree has survived countless extremes of weather over many decades and still remains strong. Its branches stretch upward and can't be blown away. When I prepare to raise my visibility as an introvert, I remind myself of the strength and majesty of the oak tree. On days that are stormy, when I feel my confidence blowing in the wind, I think of the qualities of the oak tree. I think of the relationships I've built and my strengths and accomplishments that are deeply rooted in the terra firma.

"It's important to have quiet moments of meditation and touch-stones to remind you who you are," says Rees. "These touchstones can be people, places, or things." So the oak tree is a touchstone for me (for more on meditation, see Chapter 6). Rees continues: "They may not be important to others because their importance is the meaning you ascribe to them, which is so personal. For me, it could be standing at the Palisades looking across the water to the edge of New York." (When he does, he may see your billboard!)

Certain activities can also help you get centered. I like to take a walk to gather my thoughts quietly on my own; this restores my energy—and it's something I can do almost anywhere. Some of my clients have said that they like to go for a hike or find some other connection with nature. Madeline Abel-Kerns adds: "Every morning I like to sit with my coffee and collect myself. I look over my schedule and where I am in my things to do or priorities for the month, the week, the day. In general, I collect all that information and go, 'Okay, what today?' This reduces my stress."

AFFIRMATIONS

Remember the mock self-help show called *Daily Affirmations with Stuart Smalley* on the TV show *Saturday Night Live* way back when? Political activist turned U.S. Senator Al Franken created and performed the Smalley character, whose most famous line was: "I'm good enough, I'm smart enough, and doggone it, people like me!" While we can have fun with this self-help parody, many people swear by daily affirmations. Some people say them out loud or even into a mirror, and others leave themselves positive voice-mail messages, send themselves e-mails reinforcing their strengths and accomplishments, or write positive reinforcements on Post-it® notes that they affix to their computers. In Chapter 1 I shared an affirmation that a client of mine uses. He created a laminated wallet card that says, "I can catch any ball," and several other reminders to help him get grounded. To offer another example, a colleague shares what he says to himself to help propel him forward: "My work makes the world a more humane place."

"Affirmations are phenomenal," says Anne Houle, senior manager for leadership training at Saks Fifth Avenue. "I learned about them more than 25 years ago and have been using them consistently all this time." Houle talks about how to create your own affirmation: "An affirmation works best when you make a statement using a short sentence and in the present tense. When you say your affirmation, it gives you the feeling you want to ultimately have. If it feels impossible when you say it, it's not the right affirmation."

She shares how an affirmation led to a positive change in her life: "I used an affirmation to help lead me to my current job. So if you say, 'I'm a billionaire,' your system may not accept it, but if you say, 'I am getting a high-paying job,' that's more likely to work." Houle offers a couple of creative ideas: "I put an affirmation on the screensaver on my home PC. I also wrote it on a piece of paper in big red capital letters and put it on my refrigerator." Another idea: use an affirming word or phrase in your computer passwords, since you input them multiple times a day. Maybe try something like "deep thinker"?

In the space that follows, jot down an affirmation that will help ground you.

_____

_____

_____

OFF DAYS AND UNDERSELLING YOURSELF

So with this daily self-love fest going on, how do we get thrown off balance? "The days that are hard are when I'm exhausted or not interested or feeling sour," says Abel-Kerns. "Those are the days that I have to call on the strength that says that it's okay to do nothing and just stop."

When you have off days, avoid self-defeating tendencies that can cause you to lose sight of your talents and abilities. One of these tendencies is that, as introverts, we're more inclined to undersell ourselves. According to Bob McPeek, Ph.D., director of research at the Center for Applications of Psychological Type, Inc. (CAPT): "Extroverts often get better ratings from their bosses, subordinates, and peers than introverts get—but frequently not to the degree that they rate themselves. Extroverts seem to have more self-esteem, self-acceptance, and self-confidence—a more positive self-evaluation—than introverts have."

So what do we do with this information? While you don't have to pretend you're an extrovert, consider the impact of selling yourself short. How might that affect your advancement in a competitive business environment? I'm not suggesting that you lower your standards. Instead, why not take a look at how hard you are on yourself and how much of that you signal to others? What are the consequences, and what, if anything, do you want to change? Remember that it's self-sabotaging to broadcast our imperfections in our day-to-day interactions.

COMPARING YOURSELF TO OTHERS

Another way we undermine ourselves is by wasting our energy focusing on how we measure up to others. "When I compare myself to others, that's my petty tyrant talking," says sculptor Michael Rees. "It's important to leave that at the door." Think of all of your energy contained in a large, deep bowl. When you compare yourself to others and are vulnerable to their criticism, it's as if that bowl becomes a colander and your energy escapes. "If I worry about how people are judging me, then I abandon myself," says Abel-Kerns. "When I'm on my side, trusting my own judgment, I do the best I possibly can under all circumstances." While one takeaway is to avoid comparing yourself to others, we all have times when our defenses are down. If you catch yourself slipping into unproductive comparison mode, consider this back-up strategy: use your strong points rather than your weaknesses as a point of comparison.

PROMOTING YOURSELF AUTHENTICALLY

Now that you've determined what gets you grounded, you can get more connected to your core—the part of you that's most genuine and attractive. "In the field of positive psychology, we put a big emphasis on people being authentic and using their strengths," says Senia Maymin, publisher and editor in chief of PositivePsychologyNews.com, which offers a "daily dose of research-based happiness." Maymin adds: "In fact, it's been shown that when people put on fake smiles, their hearts often have a small irregular movement at the same time, possibly from displaying an emotion that they don't feel."

Think of prominent people in any field. Then think of who promotes herself or himself authentically and who hides beneath layers of lacquer. Many of the people who are highly visible never appear to be promoting themselves—Mother Teresa comes to mind. They're passionate about their mission rather than about just getting famous. What mission are you passionate about?

"I won't succeed unless I act 100 percent who I am," says Rees. "You have to take a risk and be courageous, knowing your strengths and identifying your fire." Madeline Abel-Kerns adds: "As a teenager I created a persona that was sort of a bravado, a mask. I've always been a good actress. The introvert can hide behind the mask." Abel-Kerns shares how she's grown with respect to her mask: "It's only now that the mask is coming down and the real me is emerging. While there are times that I can still hide behind the mask, I really prefer not to now."

WHAT MAKES YOU COMFORTABLE
IN YOUR SKIN?

Authenticity connotes being comfortable in your own skin. It involves accepting who you are—your strengths as well as your challenges. "In order for me to stay comfortable in my skin, I turn my attention toward my inner self, visualize whatever I am describing in detail so that the person I am speaking to can visualize along with me, and feel the power that makes us both comfortable," says Gerceida Jones, Ph.D., who teaches fluid dynamics at New York University. Think of a time when you were most comfortable in your own skin. Where were you? What were you doing? Who, if anyone, was with you? And now, bringing this into the present: what is it about yourself that you are most comfortable with today?

YOUR BILLBOARD

Now that we've looked at your strengths from different angles and discovered ways to keep them front of mind so you can promote yourself authentically, let's do an exercise that will help you create your own personal brand. David Vinjamuri, author of *Accidental Branding*, defines the concept of branding as follows: "It's a promise— a way for consumers or other people to save time because they know that you do something better than others do it."

Remember the billboard from the beginning of this chapter? Using the affirmation you wrote as a springboard, think of a message you'd like to get across to your target audience to convey your personal brand. Madeline Abel-Kerns shares what hers would look like: "White, puffy clouds with a beautiful sky—the type of clouds you would want to sit and watch drift by, changing shapes. In black letters there would be two words: 'Be moved.' And my name and the date of my next performance."

Now it's your turn. In the space that follows write a concise headline for your billboard, draft an image (or paste in an image from a magazine). Also, write any other brief message you'd like to add, possibly to get members of your target audience who are driving by to take a desired action.

Your Billboard
Headline:
Image:
Brief message and/or action:

In the next chapter we'll get more action oriented. You'll establish a timeline for what you want to accomplish, and you'll develop an action plan for how you'll get there. You'll create a marketing mix—that is, a combination of self-promotion activities—to best support your goal and budget. While you'll consider numerous activities, you're likely to find that some are much more appealing—or less disagreeable!—than others. You'll determine what works best for you using your strengths rather than forcing yourself to do things you can't stand.

REFLECTIONS AND ACTIONS

What You Learned

1. _____

   _____

2. _____

   _____

3. _____

   _____

Action: What will you do?	How You'll Do It: What support or further information will you obtain?	Accountability: Whom will you tell about this action?	Completion Date: By when?

three

Your Game Plan

Creating a Winning Marketing Mix

If you were just like everyone out there, I'd recommend a one-size-fits-all approach to raising your visibility. However, since you're unique, why not find ways to promote yourself that work best for your personality and preferences? Just because a gregarious colleague glad-hands her way through every social function doesn't mean that's what you should do. In fact, as an introvert, you may feel foolish glad-handing. You'd probably do better by playing to your strengths, which are more likely to include building deep, lasting relationships, researching, thinking before you speak, and gaining expertise. These activities can help you raise your visibility while also benefiting your stakeholders. Of course, self-promotion—at least the way we're practicing it in this book—is never just about you; it's also about how you can help others by offering them something they'll value. But first they have to know about you, and it's your job to make sure that happens.

In this chapter you'll identify your self-promotion goals and craft a game plan that fits your schedule and budget as well as your temperament. Planning is a power tool for many of us introverts because it enables us to go inward and think quietly behind the scenes before we act or speak. Even if you're not naturally a planner, you'll find plenty of activities and ideas to help you advance your self-promotion efforts your way. You'll devise a custom combination of self-promotion activities, or a marketing mix. Pick the activities that you like best—or find least objectionable!—and become the steward of your own visibility.

MY WAY

Self-promotion doesn't have to be a nasty-tasting medicine. Reframe it as a game you can enjoy playing, one whose rules are fluid and that both parties can win at. I don't exhaust myself by pushing or taking things personally when people say no. I just present myself authentically, again and again, until I get the desired yes. But first I have to say yes to myself.

I've never written a book before, so saying yes to myself meant shoehorning a seemingly impossible number of extra hours into an already full schedule. Compounding that was my morbid phobia of writing—on a blank page, anyhow. I could have let my negative self-talk convince me that I'm an intellectual invalid who can't even string a sentence together, but since I don't put up with such trash talk from anyone else, why should I from myself?

While I didn't initially write down a master plan, I played to my strengths as an experienced project manager and networker while also tackling the hardest part: getting myself to sit down and write. I broke down my deliverables into small chunks, which I wrote on my daily to-do list. I built in plenty of room for road bumps, like lost computer files, accidentally erased interview tapes, and unreturned phone calls as well as time to reflect at interim points. While I do my best thinking alone, there's no way I could write a book without support and input from others. As Simi Sanni Nwogugu, CEO of HOD Consulting, Inc., a diversity consulting organization, notes: "I have faced many challenges in my career, and have found that I do best when I bounce ideas around with a lot of people and then retreat into my own private space to think about what I gathered and put it in a logical structure."

An extroverted author tells me that she writes her books from start to finish and never looks back. Not me—I scour every sentence. She would find it intolerable to work my way, and vice versa. We're wired differently, and so our ways of getting things done are quite different. While I rarely follow a straight path, I've learned to embrace my loops and squiggles. So am I goal oriented? Yes and no. I pay attention to the research, listen to my intuition, seek expert input, and then do things my way. Now let's find your way.

THE ARGUMENT FOR GOALS

You may not be particularly goal oriented. Maybe you would prefer to take it a day at a time, or just experience life in a loose and nimble flow. That's fine, especially if you're highly intuitive, fast on your feet, or just lucky. However, if you're not always in the right place at the right time and you'd like to get someplace more desirable in your career, take a stab at the exercises and action plan in this chapter, even if you do so only in your head. Give them a test drive. They are likely to guide you toward someplace you want to go.

> Wandering and playing are great—allowing your brain to take a vacation and dream. Here's where destination comes in: "I want to go to Italy. I might get there eventually by wandering, but if I know how to get there and track it, I will get there more quickly."
> —**Jeanine Tesori, award-winning composer of the Broadway musicals *Caroline, or Change* and *Thoroughly Modern Millie***

"Research has compellingly found that if someone wants to achieve a performance goal, it should be challenging, specific, measurable, and due by a deadline," says Caroline Adams Miller, author, motivational speaker, and professional coach. "Without specific goals we are all prone to be somewhat reactive instead of proactive, which isn't conducive to change and growth." Miller points out: "The healthiest type of growth involves setting goals that take us outside our comfort zone so we learn how to experience risks that pay off handsomely with rewards. Playing it safe," she says, "doesn't have the same payoff. In fact, some of the newest research out of the University of British Columbia by Dr. Jessica Tracy has found that authentic self-esteem is fostered by taking on challenging goals that require doing something hard and outside one's comfort zone.

"Finally," adds Miller, "goal setting and goal accomplishment are traits of happy people. We can all shift our biological set point by going after short- and long-term goals that are tied in with our values." Miller describes the payoff: "Once we do this, we begin to experience some of the benefits of frequent positive affect, which include better relationships, more energy, more optimism, better health, and more resilience in the face of stress."

Reflect on how you've achieved the accomplishments you're most proud of. Did you aim for them, or were they a result of serendipity? Did you spend many years studying and researching to attain them? Or were you in the right place at the right time? Are you concerned that if you put too much emphasis on a particular goal, you'll set yourself up for failure? How about the notion of just trying your best without setting a goal? Research reported in the *American Psychologist* shows that "when people are asked to do their best, they do not do so."[1] What insights have you had about goal setting at this point?

Goals and Accountability

A funny thing happens to many of my coaching clients even before our first session. From the day they commit to getting coached, they begin to focus more and take steps toward their self-promotion goals. I wonder if they also straighten up before the housekeeper comes! Many find it challenging to move toward their goals without deadlines that they commit to others. I can relate. As much as I've always wanted to write a book, it took signing a contract to get me in gear. Can you relate?

The key is knowing yourself, as basketball legend and author of *32 Ways to Be a Champion in Business* Earvin "Magic" Johnson describes in Chapter 2—and acting on that knowledge. If you work best under deadline pressure, then get yourself on a deadline. If you work better with the support or camaraderie of another individual or a small group, then get that support rather than fighting what you know you need. Don't waste your energy comparing yourself to all the self-motivated Michelangelos you know and wishing that you were different.

Snack-Sized Goals

One of my students at New York University shares that she's adept at planning her self-promotion efforts—in fact, she can make lists all day. The hard part is turning the plans into actions. So how do we do that? Award-winning composer Jeanine Tesori says she learned from working with kids to make each step snack-sized. "Create a design and write it down," she advises. "Determine the stepping stones to help you get there. That's my process when I write. I think of the end result I want and then work backward. Introverts get overwhelmed," she continues, "by so many choices of things to say and things to do. Just get it down and make it smaller. It becomes more doable, and the goal feels more attainable."

Cathie Black, president of Hearst Magazines, addresses how to apply this advice at work: "Take on small things that allow you to feel good about yourself. Volunteer to work on a special project. To reduce the risk, you don't have to be in charge of it. Work with a small team. They'll begin to see that you're smart and you've got something to add to the conversation." She points out: "You don't have to have a big win. Instead, build your confidence with little wins. String together several of them, and you'll walk down the street with poise and confidence."

While it's fine to stretch, avoid making unrealistic demands on yourself. If a mantra would be helpful, think *chunking*. While it has so many disparate meanings—from a large city in central China to a brand used by ConAgra for shelf-stable foods to a method used in computational linguistics—to me, *chunking* is the act of breaking things down into smaller pieces so I don't get overwhelmed. So many priorities are always looming with so little time to tackle them. Chunking things down makes them all the more manageable.

Promoting Friends and Colleagues Also Benefits You

One day I received an e-mail that stood out in my inbox. Michele Wucker, executive director of the World Policy Institute, a global think tank, was promoting books her friends and colleagues had recently written. In doing so, she was not only bringing these new resources to the attention of people in her circle, but just by sending the e-mail, she was also reminding me to think of her. She set up a section on her Web site and Facebook page called "Michele's Bookshelf," another place where she promotes other authors' books. You can learn about the books she's written there too.

THE ARGUMENT AGAINST GOALS

Even goals have their detractors. "I've always had trouble with the idea of overarching *goals*," says actor and longtime New York TV anchor Brad Holbrook. "People constantly ask about your goals, especially when you're young and starting out." He shares from his own experience: "I always aimed to perform whatever task was at hand the best I could, and that would create opportunities. Larger success would be generated by smaller successes.

"There is a danger in trying to manipulate your unfolding career path too much," he adds. "You set yourself up for needless disappointment if things don't work out exactly as you had envisioned. My feelings about 'The Big Goal' may go back to my days as a baseball player in high school. Everyone's goals are the same in sports: win the game. Make the play, go with the right decision, and give maximum effort—at every opportunity. The game, the season, and the honors then take care of themselves. I always look at it from the perspective of my baseball playing past: as a hitter, if you're successful 3 times out of 10, you go to the Hall of Fame!"

The idea of setting and moving toward your goals, particularly as they relate to self-promotion, may intimidate you, or even sound too formal and rigid. I'll offer you a variety of ways to think about goals and action plans. We'll talk about how you can relate to your goals as friendly focal points rather than foes and how just the act of setting a goal can help take you a step in its direction.

"Remember that we are the bosses of our goals and dreams, and not the other way around," says Marianna Lead, Ph.D., founder of Goal Imagery® Institute and former president of the International Coach Federation, New York City chapter. "We should not feel imprisoned by them. My workshop participants are often shocked to discover not only that they have the power to change their goals, but that it's okay to feel good about it. There's a difference between giving up and simply changing direction."

HOW TO BEST TACKLE CHALLENGES

It's time for action—planning action, anyhow. I created a quick and fun exercise to get you thinking about how you best tackle challenges. In the space that follows, write a brief description of a challenge that you've successfully tackled. You could summarize how you designed and implemented a plan to cut costs by 30 percent in your business, or how you reorganized your office space to be more conducive to your thinking process. Write anything that demonstrates your problem-solving acumen—it doesn't have to be about self-promotion.

_____

_____

_____

Reflect on what you wrote. Identify which of your strengths—introverted or otherwise—you used to solve the problem. If you'd like a quick reminder of your strengths, refer to the ones that you listed in Chapter 2. What's your style of tackling challenges? Are you a plotter-planner? An intuitive problem solver? A collaborator? How about a fire extinguisher?

Holding a Reception Thanking the Team

One of the best ways to toot your own horn when you've done something really well on a team project—even though you may have done most of the work—is to hold a reception thanking your team and invite your bosses. By doing that, you achieve two things. You get your boss to focus attention on the really good job you did, and you also put your boss in a position to thank the others on the team, which then plays on many levels.

—Kathleen Waldron, Ph.D., president of Baruch College

Now for something a little more challenging. The exercise in the table that follows will get you to think about your self-promotion goals in different ways. Of course, self-promotion goals may not be something that comes readily to your mind. While you may want to be as renowned as Albert Einstein, more likely you want to attain a certain level of visibility to achieve what you want in your life.

Meet artist-author Nicole Titus, a clinical supervisor in the medical department at a Fortune 500 company who took an early retirement package so she could dedicate herself to fighting illiteracy, which is currently at 50 percent in her native country, Haiti. "I created a program in which incentives are used to achieve 100 percent literacy in poor Haitian communities, namely by feeding the children and giving them a small stipend daily," she says. "Children teach other children in this program. One of the ways I raise funds is by auctioning off my artwork. I have to get out of my comfort zone to address large audiences, which does not come easily for me as an introvert." Titus's lifetime goal is to end illiteracy as well as child labor, which is also rampant in Haiti. Now let's talk about attaining your goals.

YOUR SELF-PROMOTION GOALS

In the first row of the table that follows, write your self-promotion goals for each of the time frames specified. Then, in the rows below, jot down your thoughts about different aspects of attaining your short- and long-term self-promotion goals. See what insights come up for you.

A self-promotion goal that seems small to one person may be formidable to another. Whether your goal this week is to send an e-mail to network with an old colleague or to plan an event you can host, be sure it's within your reach, no matter how easy you think it may be for someone else, particularly Jo(e) Extrovert. If your goals are too outsized, you run the risk of getting overwhelmed and spiraling downward into inaction. Not that inaction is necessarily a problem. Sometimes sitting tight can give you a chance to catch your breath—as long as you can manage your negative self-talk during those times when you're not actually "doing" something. After all, for an introvert, thinking is often an important precursor to doing.

Determine Your Self-Promotion Goals

	This Week	This Month	This Year
Your self-promotion goal			
Ease or difficulty of attaining each self-promotion goal (1 = very easy; 2 = easy; 3 = doable; 4 = difficult; 5 = very difficult)			
Desired results of attaining each goal			
One thing you're likely to enjoy about the process			
One thing you're likely to enjoy about the outcome			
Possible stumbling blocks			
How to prevent and/or manage the stumbling blocks			
What kind of support you'll need to attain each goal			
Whom you can contact to get advice, insight, or other assistance			
What resources would be helpful			
Other thoughts			

Next Year	In 5 Years	In 10 Years	In Your Lifetime

YOUR MARKETING MIX

Now that you've set—or at least penciled in—your short- and long-term self-promotion goals, it's time for you to create a marketing mix that will consist of the activities you can choose to reach these goals. Start by jotting down, on top of the table that follows, one of the self-promotion goals you just described; also write down the target audiences you'll need to reach to attain that goal. Then look at the long, but by no means exhaustive, list of self-promotion activities I've compiled for you to consider. I offer different perspectives and tips about some of these activities later in this chapter in the section titled "Self-Promotion Picks for Introverts."

"While the list of self-promotion things you don't want to do as an introvert probably outweighs the things you're willing to do," says Heidi Rome, marketing director, UJA-Federation of New York, "you still have plenty to choose from. Plus, it's always smart to reevaluate and resist that inner comfort zone. I've often surprised myself by changing my mind and trying something new I may have resisted before."

On that note, rate each of the self-promotion activities based on your personal preferences and your past experiences. So if you like conducting seminars and strongly dislike cold calling, it's clear which one of those to include in your marketing mix.

Once you've rated all of the self-promotion activities listed, pick five (or more if you're an energetic introvert!) that most effectively play to your strengths and preferences. This is your marketing mix. Keep in mind that self-promotion activities, like the components of any good marketing campaign, usually require multiple repeats to get your target audiences' attention, let alone their buy-in. Think about how many times you need to be exposed to something or someone before you are sold.

Create Your Marketing Mix

Your self-promotion goal (pick one): _____

Your target audiences: _____

Rate your preferences for the self-promotion activities below on a scale of 1 to 5
(1 = strongly like; 2 = like; 3 = neutral; 4 = dislike; and 5 = strongly dislike).

Self-Promotion Activity	1	2	3	4	5
Web site					
Advertising and/or posting on other Web sites					
Blogging and microblogging (e.g., Twitter)					
Podcasts and videocasts					
Online groups (e.g., Yahoo.com)					
Job listings and research (e.g., www.craigslist.com, www.careerbuilder.com)					
Other classified ads (in print and online)					
Flyers					
Brochures					
Postcards					
Coupons and/or gift certificates					
Yellow Pages display ads					
Professional and alumni publications and directories					
Advertising free or low-cost samples of your work or special package deals					
Direct mail (Consider using a personalized postage stamp with your likeness!)					
Individualized letters and/or e-mails					
Public relations efforts (e.g., press releases)					

Self-Promotion Activity	1	2	3	4	5
Free phone consultations					
Free reports or white papers					
Do-it-yourself guides					
Newsletters—e-mail or hard copy					
Joining nonprofit board of directors					
Advertising specialty items (e.g., imprinted pens)					
Surveys and/or questionnaires					
Articles in trade and other publications					
Op-ed pieces and letters to the editor					
Speakers' bureaus					
Networking events (e.g., gatherings of professional organizations, Chambers of Commerce, Meetup.com)					
Informational interviews with colleagues, prospective clients, and employers					
Radio talk shows					
Teaching adult education courses					
Conducting teleconferences, seminars, or webinars					
Setting up a booth at a fair or conference					
Audio recordings of educational information					
Cold calling					
Auctioning off your services at a charity event					
Other:					

Now that you've rated these self-promotion activities, circle five or more that will make up your marketing mix. Take a moment to reflect, and on the line below, write down one insight you've had by doing this exercise:

Did you pick mostly familiar activities or new ones? Did you pick activities that could tap into your introverted strengths, such as writing and researching, or did you fill in the blanks with wild stretch assignments, like crashing an inaugural ball just to challenge yourself?

Self-Promotion Tips and Reminders

Keep the following tips and reminders front of mind whenever you engage in self-promotion activities:

- Whether you're writing or speaking, before you say a word, start by putting yourself in your audience's shoes and answering: What's In It For Me?—or WIIFM. We'll take a closer look at this time-tested concept in Chapter 4, when we talk about targeting your audience.
- Make your messages crisp, clear, and concise. While the length of the average attention span of an adult is much contested, think of your own attention for other people's self-promotion speeches. Mine is often less than a minute.
- Try out your self-promotion messages—from your elevator pitch (more about that in Chapter 5) to the content of your promotional e-mails—on a test group that resembles one of your target audiences, and welcome feedback.
- Follow through on all leads, and circle back appreciatively to those who make introductions for you; apprise them, in particular, of positive outcomes.
- If you're not a good writer, take a class or hire (or barter with) someone to do your promotional writing.
- If your public speaking abilities need work, take a class, join Toastmasters International, or hire a public speaking coach.
- Practice speaking in sound bites, and use your introverted strengths to listen carefully to your conversation partners.

People You Know in the News

Google your name. Do you like the quality and quantity of mentions you get? This is what your employers and clients see when they search for your name. "A great way to keep track of information that might interest your contacts, as well as what they're up to, is using Google News Alerts," according to Ben Dattner, Ph.D., workplace consultant and adjunct professor of industrial and organizational psychology at New York University. Likewise, I recommend setting up a Google News Alert for your own name to see whenever it pops up in the public domain.

YOUR GAME PLAN

Now that you've laid the groundwork, it's time to create a personalized game plan. Let's focus on what you can do best with the least effort for the biggest payoff, rather than on what makes you cringe. You'll map out when you're going to do each of the self-promotion activities you chose from the Create Your Marketing Mix table. Whether you do that on a complex spreadsheet, on a cocktail napkin, or in your head, this is the place to give deep thought—an introverted strength!—to the steps you'll take toward your goal. You'll design a game plan with the right level of detail and flexibility for you.

I'll offer you tips to help you manage three of the ubiquitous self-promotion biggies: time, energy, and money. Maybe it's because I live in New York, but I don't know anyone who thinks she or he has too much time or money. So unless you're reading this while lazing on your own private island or are planning an outpost in space donning your name, let's create the most buzz for your buck.

While I initially suggested that you create a marketing mix requiring the "least effort" for the greatest return, I didn't mean to imply "no effort." "Building your career is building your life," says Broadway legend Chita Rivera, "because career and life are not separated." She adds: "Work hard—really don't think it comes easy, because nothing comes easy." Since raising your visibility is an important part of building your career, you need to work hard at that too. However, you can save your energy—an often limited resource for introverts—by gaining clarity about your offerings, whom you're targeting, and what's in it for them. You'll also avoid lots of annoying, fruitless activities that might even backfire because they are better suited to extroverts. "It's about self-motivation," says Laurie Graff, actor and author of *The Shiksa Syndrome: A Novel.* "You're the captain of your own team. Look inside yourself. Be clear about what you really *want* to do." That clarity will illuminate your path and help you navigate the road-blocks you may encounter.

Raising Your Visibility While Making a Difference

What do you need to do to make a difference in your life and in the lives of others? Regardless of which causes you're passionate about, there's plenty you can do to help. Meet Karen Dawn, author of *Thanking the Monkey: Rethinking the Way We Treat Animals.* By writing her book, participating in numerous press interviews, and teaching animal advocates how to work with the media to get their message out, Dawn's name has become inextricable from her message; she believes that caring for the earth and its animals is part of caring for ourselves and each other. "I am passionate about this cause," she says. "You can't get the message out there if you're unwilling to get yourself out there. Devote your energy to making a difference. Put the message above your own sense of discomfort. When you're working for a cause you care about, it's easier to do that."

YOUR TIME AND ENERGY

I don't know about you, but if I have to do a task I don't enjoy or that doesn't play to my strengths (e.g., cold calling), I'm a jumping bean. I sit down to do it and then realize that I really need to water my plants, polish my shoes, and wax my floors. Then I skid down the hall to make a cup of tea. I'll do anything to escape a dreaded task that I "should" do, but just don't wanna do (arms folded, stomp, harrumph). That's why I asked you to rate the tasks in your marketing mix and pick the ones you like the most.

It's important to manage your time and energy as an introvert. Once again, a one-size-fits-all approach is unlikely to work. Here are some basics and reminders to help you keep your balance.

Keep Your Balance

Do

1. Schedule realistically, being mindful of your energy. Think about how many and what kinds of tasks you can accomplish in a day without getting drained.
2. Plan on downtime between social interactions.
3. Build in time to prepare for meetings.
4. Include activities in your marketing mix that play to your introverted strengths.
5. Get the support you need (e.g., from a virtual assistant, mentor, coach, professional organization) to help you make your game plan even more doable. One effective approach is to start or join a *mastermind group*, which is a gathering of people who share resources and advice and act as a sounding board for each other, all toward a definite purpose—say, career advancement. You can read more about the concept in the writings of Napoleon Hill, author of the celebrated *Think and Grow Rich*. You can also get a taste for the concept on the Napoleon Hill Foundation's Web site at www.naphill.org.

Don't

1. Plan lots of social activities and meetings back to back.
2. Compare yourself to extroverts, who manage their time and activities differently from you.

3. Get down on yourself for not having as much energy for social interaction as others.
4. Put yourself in situations that require you to speak impromptu without time to catch your breath and prepare.
5. Give up—believe in yourself and trust that you'll find your path.

Stay focused on your goals and tackle your priorities first, rather than getting bogged down with the less important stuff. You can choose from myriad personal organizers if those tools are helpful to you—from Filofaxes to BlackBerrys to online calendars on Outlook, Google, and so on. What do you gravitate to most?

Time Management, My Way

While I've tried many approaches, I've realized that I need a system that's closely mapped to the way I think. I find that my handwriting speaks to me much better than the printed word. So I put my daily appointments, important notes, and deliverables into a personal digital assistant (PDA); I use that as a central repository and, in some ways, as an auxiliary brain that keeps track of all those endless details. Then I print out my schedule the night before for the following day. I review it and make handwritten notes in the margins.

Why not just handwrite the notes to begin with? My method (or madness!) is twofold: I keep my appointments and deliverables in one easily searchable electronic place, while also getting the benefit of my scribble, which takes the express lane to my brain. You can do it your way.

To take the next step, use a blank monthly calendar to get you started and to help you visualize your plan for the year. Write in holidays, vacations, and other major events in your life to help you get a better picture of your available time. You can also factor in how much energy you're likely to have to tackle the self-promotion activities in your marketing mix. The process of creating this calendar will probably lead to some insights. While you may want to create a more detailed plan using a different approach, this preliminary activity will get you started.

On the calendar, pencil in the self-promotion activities you circled on the Create Your Marketing Mix table. If you chose, for example, direct mail, write on the calendar each time you'd like to send out a mailer—say January, March, June, and September. If you also chose to conduct seminars, write on the calendar when you'd like to do so, and so on.

MONEY

While many of your self-promotion efforts can be free, some can cost money, and some can even pay. The freebies can include blogging, producing a podcast, and creating a press release. The ones that cost money include placing advertisements and buying mailing lists for promotional mailers. The ones that pay include some public speaking gigs and selling articles you write. Instead of the basic calendar that we just created, you can create a spreadsheet to track what your self-promotion activities will cost and what revenues they can bring you.

While we're on the topic of money, if you chose some form of advertising as part of your marketing mix, keep in mind that advertising usually takes repeat exposure to the right audiences over time; while it can be effective, it can also cost a good deal of money. If that doesn't sound right for you or you can't afford it right now, then find other ways to get your name out there. If advertising makes sense for you, then spend your money carefully. Assess the various places you can advertise, both on the Web and in traditional media, and come up with a plan that works within your budget.

Did I say budget? If you choose activities that cost money, consider making a budget to correspond with your self-promotion game plan. If this sounds daunting, you're not alone. It's hard to find people who are relaxed and clear about their personal finances. In fact, a poll by the American Psychological Association (APA) found that 75 percent of Americans are stressed about money.[2] If budgeting doesn't play to your strengths, learn more from books and resources on the Web, or ask someone more knowledgeable for assistance. Here's one Web site with a wealth of information and links: www.shoestringmag.com. If your financial resources are tight, make a barter deal with someone you know or place an ad on craigslist. You can also start or join an in-person or online group to learn more about personal or small-business finance.

SELF-PROMOTION PICKS FROM INTROVERTS

With a laundry list of self-promotion activities to choose from, I hope it helped to select five of your favorites for your marketing mix. Now we'll take a closer look at some activities that work well for some introverts. See which ones appeal to you after reading more about them. Feel free to adjust your marketing mix until you find the right combination of activities that play to your strengths and that are effective at reaching your target audiences. It will probably take some trial and error over time.

Networking

I've long sworn by networking, which I define as building relationships over time for mutual benefit. "I can thank my network for some of the greatest career opportunities of my life," says Pamela Skillings, author of *Escape from Corporate America*. "Hard work and talent are important. However, if you maintain a strong network, they'll take you a lot further. Networking is the key to finding the very best job leads, job recommendations, advice, introductions, and more."

While it takes time to cultivate these relationships, it doesn't cost a lot of money. Sure, I pick up the bill sometimes when I meet people in my network for coffee, lunch, or drinks, and I pay to go to certain events. However, most of my networking just requires a phone and Internet connection to stay in touch, show interest, introduce people, and solve their problems. You'll find a more in-depth discussion about networking in Chapter 5.

Press

I've been fortunate to receive favorable press attention when I've run my own businesses. I just let journalists know what I'm doing that's newsworthy, respond immediately and thoroughly to their inquiries, serve as a useful source, and introduce them to other sources. The same journalists have returned for more interviews because they know they can rely on me to reply quickly with sound bites they can use.

"I was a reporter for my college newspaper," says Ben Dattner, Ph.D., "so I tap into my inner journalist. I genuinely enjoy speaking with journalists, pitching to them, and assisting them, even when they can't quote me. A lot of people don't realize how hard their job is—particularly those covering something like the workplace in a weekly or monthly column. It's hard to find new workplace trends every week or month. So even if you're not pitching yourself, it can be helpful if you pitch them your ideas." Dattner, a workplace consultant and an adjunct professor of industrial and organizational psychology at New York University, is big on building relationships: "I hosted a lunch last week and invited 15 workplace journalists. It gave them a chance to meet each other." It's no surprise he's a frequent guest on national TV and radio shows and is often quoted in major print and online media.

"Introverts can get press coverage by being persistent, reaching out, and just being the authentic wonderful people that they are," says Annie Hoffman, an Emmy Award–nominated broadcaster who has interviewed everyone from Serena Williams to Jerry Seinfeld. "It's so important that you're passionate about what you do because the press people you pitch to can read between the lines. Your mouth can be going, but if you don't really believe in what you're saying, they'll pick up on it."

Hoffman, also a TV producer and a cofounder of Sportscast Stars Training, recommends building relationships with newspapers and with local TV and radio stations. "Pitch ideas to them, invite them to your functions and to lunch, and hold press conferences," she says. "If the thought of holding a press conference is daunting for you as an introvert, you can learn about it from books, Web sites, adult education courses, and specialized coaches and trainers." She offers a note of encouragement: "It's so easy to send out press releases, which you can do inexpensively on the Web. If you're not a good writer, find a friend or graduate student studying communications at a local college who is."

"Local radio is a particularly good outlet," Hoffman adds. "You could, depending on what your business is, offer [a local station] something to give out on the air, or possibly tie into a promotion for the station. Let's say that you're a restaurant—deliver things to the morning show. They love food."

Hoffman recommends making it as easy as possible for your press contacts to give you good ink. "Map out everything, and supply them with photos and interviews with other people," she says. "I just media trained up-and-coming race car drivers. Some lamented that they didn't have a PR person. Until they're able to hire one, I told them that they could act as their own PR people by just learning some basics. For example, I recommended that they work with their local media and offer winter driving tips. While that may sound a little cheesy, it works. Ultimately," Hoffman concludes, "the race car drivers gain a greater understanding and appreciation for what a PR person needs to do in order to success-fully market them."

What do you do when press people don't return your calls? "Don't be offended. Just keep trying," says Hoffman. "They're often doing the jobs of three people. Make your message concrete and help them as much as you can. The more you do so, the more likely the story is going to run. If the media people don't bite, tweak your message, give it a few months, and try again."

Help a Reporter Out (HARO)

Would you like to help a reporter find an excellent source for an article she or he is writing? That source may be you, or even some-one in your network whom you'd like to help. "HARO connects journalists and sources totally for free under the belief that every-one is an expert at something," says its founder Peter Shankman. I subscribe to daily e-mails from HARO, which contain a list of queries from journalists writing articles on everything from social media business mistakes to how to spot a foreclosure rescue scam. Sooner or later a journalist at a news outlet will be looking for someone with your expertise. Sign up for a free subscription at www.helpareporter.com.

How to Give a Great Press Interview

Steve Orr, a MarketWatch Radio Network anchor, has interviewed hundreds of people including CEOs, politicians, authors, analysts, athletes, and celebrities during his more than 20 years in radio and TV broadcasting. He offers the following tips—many of which draw on your introverted strengths—for how you can best work with the press:

1. Be prepared. Different reporters will look for different angles. Let's say you're a CEO and you've just written a book about your life and career. A business reporter might be more interested in how you rose through the ranks, from slinging envelopes in the mailroom to becoming a chief executive; on the other hand, a style section reporter may be more interested in how growing up as the son of a Marine captain shaped your values. As an introvert, you might be most comfortable anticipating the types of questions you'll be asked, and then rehearsing them. Plan for the usual *who, what, where, when, why,* and *how* questions. Also plan for questions that come out of left field, such as, "Why were you wearing a Hawaiian shirt and a pith helmet at the meeting?" The trick is to be flexible enough to handle questions you don't think you'll be asked, and practicing answers to gain confidence.

2. Be concise.   Let's say a friend asked you what you did this morning. You might say, "I woke up at 7 a.m., rubbed my eyes, got out of bed slowly, went to the bathroom, splashed some water on my face, and spotted a pink elephant sunning on my lawn." If it's a press interview, all you need to say is, "I spotted a pink elephant sunning on my lawn." That's editing, and that's what's newsworthy. If it's not a live interview, reporters will have control over what they use from you and how they use it—if at all. They're often under very tight deadlines. Keep your answers under 30 seconds; they'll be more likely to use them—and call you again. Introverts: Practice is essential. Get a stop watch and time yourself giving a brief response.

3. Know your audience.   Ask the reporter who the story is targeting and then tailor your remarks. Wouldn't your language be different when addressing a group of fifth graders than a group of rocket scientists? Also, avoid industry jargon to save reporters from asking you for clarification. Tell a reporter why something is significant and why the audience should care in simple, straightforward language.

4. Answer the question you're asked. Too often people—especially politicians—answer the question they want asked rather than the question that is asked. Use your introvert's propensity to listen carefully. Others may have advised you to do the opposite and to make your message heard, regardless of what the reporter wants or needs. That's wasting a reporter's time. No reporter wants to keep asking the same question several different ways to get an answer—especially on a live interview. That reporter will surely not call you again. When you listen to the questions, chances are you'll be able to work your talking points into the answers. Often at the end of an interview, reporters will ask if there's anything else you'd like to add. That's your opportunity to bring up something you haven't yet covered.

5. Be relaxed. Introverts usually aren't crazy about speaking impromptu. If you're tense, chances are you'll speak too fast, you won't breathe normally, your voice will sound strained, and your pitch may even go up. Also, don't speak in a monotone. The more natural your voice sounds, the more likely you'll get airtime on radio or TV as well as capture the attention of a newspaper reporter who's asking you questions.

6. Never read from a press release. They're not meant to be read out loud. Practice delivering your message conversationally. Audio- or video-tape yourself to fine-tune your delivery.

7. Be engaged. Close your office door and turn your phone off so you won't be distracted during the interview. If you're interviewed in person, maintain eye contact with the reporter. Be personable and passionate, even if it's the tenth time you've told the same anecdote.

8. Be nonconfrontational. Don't snap at your interviewer. Years ago, I had the misfortune of asking a legendary jazz singer a perfectly innocuous question that she didn't like. She was easily in her seventies at the time, and I certainly had no reason to grill her.

She snapped at me, and the interview, which lasted only a minute or so longer, quickly went downhill. She got away with it because she was an icon. However, I don't recommend that you do it. If you snap or lose your temper, it might make great theater, but you could damage your reputation and credibility.

9. Offer facts and figures. Journalists love statistics, but make them brief and easily understandable. That will give your stats a better chance of being used.

10. Call right back. Keep in mind that reporters are often under tight deadlines. Always call them back as soon as possible. If they don't hear from you, sometimes within minutes, they'll move on to someone else.

TV Interviews

Michele Wucker, executive director of the World Policy Institute, a global think tank, shares what it was like for her, as an introvert, to appear on live national TV. "In a weird way," she notes, "the awkward setup that most TV interviews entail is actually good for introverts. You're alone in a little room with an earpiece in your ear and a little camera in front of you, behind a closed door."

Public Speaking

Public speaking is an efficient way for an introvert to raise her or his visibility. If it sounds like a frightening means to an end, it doesn't have to be. Help is available; you can conquer your fear of public speaking with the right support. I developed my public speaking skills by doing pro bono presentations, and after a short while, I was able to charge a fee. I got elected to boards of directors at professional organizations—volunteer positions that enabled me to develop strong relationships for mutual referrals, collaborations, valuable information, and more speaking opportunities. You don't have to do stump speeches to qualify as a public speaker. Start small and see where it takes you. For a more in-depth discussion on public speaking and presentation skills, see Chapter 6.

Writing

While writing doesn't come easily to me, I like that I can edit privately, on my own time. It's a safe way to communicate for an introvert. Getting published, whether it's in a newsletter, a book, or a blog, is a smart way to benefit many people by sharing your expertise while also raising your visibility.

David Vinjamuri, author of *Accidental Branding*, says: "Writing enhances your personal brand by positioning you as an expert. Writing a book has had multiple downstream benefits for me. I've gotten a lot more speaking engagements and media coverage. I'm also now writing regularly for *Brandweek*, I'm a regular guest on *Fox Business News*, and I've gotten new clients."

Kathleen Waldron, Ph.D., president of Baruch College, offers a creative idea: "Early in my career, I went to a senior person and we cowrote a one-pager for one of the trade journals. I did most of the work and he worked on it also, but it was clearly a coauthorship. It really was very self-promoting for me to do it, and in a non-threatening way. Of course, I linked my name to a more senior person's—and he and I just traded career opportunities. I helped him, he helped me, and we're still in touch 20 years later."

Op-Eds

Op-eds are perfect for anyone who likes to think, write, and express her views; they're also a great way to raise your visibility. So they're ideal for introverts. Several women I know have enthusiastically recommended The OpEd Project; its Web site (www.theopedproject.org) says that it "trains women experts across the nation to project their voices on the op-ed pages of major newspapers and other key forums of public discourse." According to Catherine Orenstein, the founder of The OpEd Project, women tend to shy away from claiming to be experts. My experience working with introverts—women and men alike—is similar. We often undersell how much we know. While women can directly benefit from The OpEd Project and its sister resource, www.SheSource. org, which is a repository of women experts, any introvert can get inspired by the idea and write an op-ed.

Referrals

As a coach, much of my business is through referrals. I take care of my clients, and they spread the word for me. I also get referrals from friends, colleagues, and former managers. What are your sources of referrals? Who can write letters of recommendation and testimonials for your promotional materials?

Social Media

Social media offer additional possibilities for you to expand your horizons while sitting at your computer. Blogs, message boards, wikis, and Yahoo! and Google groups enable you to write to people and share ideas; podcasts and YouTube let you broadcast your message to a potentially large audience; and social networking sites, like LinkedIn, Facebook, and Twitter, let you share information and stay informed. Of course, sites can gain massive popularity almost overnight, so watch for new ones that may crop up.

We'll discuss how you can use social media to raise your visibility in the pages that follow. Meanwhile, if you're just getting up the learning curve, check out the fun and instructive YouTube video titled "LinkedIn in Plain English" (there are also videos for Twitter, wikis, and RSS) created by Lee LeFever and Sachi LeFever—their Web site is www.commoncraft.com.

Introverts and Our Keyboards

"Studies are finding that introverts are a significant force behind the emergence of social media, including blogs, social networks, and other user-generated content," says Rick Lavoie, senior account director at Critical Mass, a digital marketing agency. Many of us prefer to spend more time sitting at our keyboards than interacting face-to-face. Online interactions not only enable us to gather our thoughts, take the time to edit, and share our ideas when we're ready; they also help us reach many more people than we'd have energy for when working a room, pounding the pavement, or even making cold calls. While face-to-face and online approaches to marketing yourself are not mutually exclusive, it's easier for us introverts to rely more on digital media to get the job done.

Which of the digital media do you gravitate to for your various communication needs? How about your audiences? "Talking has become a rarity," says a client of mine we'll call Genevieve Menard, an executive assistant at an investment bank. "In the Midtown skyscraper where I work, I run into corporate lawyers, marketing executives, and financial executives every day. They're busy looking down at their BlackBerrys and cell phones whenever they step out of the office. Even their secretaries have BlackBerrys. On most mornings I'm greeted by silence when I step into the packed elevator." So as a nation, we're becoming all thumbs!

How do we spread our message and raise our visibility using digital media? "It's not about driving people to your Web site anymore. Instead, it's about engaging in conversations with your audience by blogging, generating content on sites such as YouTube, and social networking on sites such as LinkedIn. Your audiences will not only become aware of you. They'll also see the value of your contributions," says Lavoie. So introverts, our time has come!

Who's Watching

Just as you would in traditional networking situations, consider the image you want to get across in the arena of social networking. Maintaining a professional presence on social networking sites can give you an edge over the competition when you're seeking a job. A nationwide CareerBuilder.com survey of more than 3,100 employers found that 22 percent of hiring managers use social networking sites to research candidates, and an additional 9 percent plan on doing so. Furthermore, of those who researched candidates on these sites, 24 percent found content that helped solidify their decision to hire the candidate, and 34 percent found content causing them to dismiss the candidate from consideration. Top areas of concern included candidates' posting information about their drinking or using drugs (41 percent), posting provocative or inappropriate photographs or information (40 percent), exhibiting poor communication skills (29 percent), bad-mouthing their previous company or fellow employee (28 percent), lying about qualifications (27 percent), and making discriminatory remarks related to such characteristics as race, gender, or religion (22 percent). Other faux pas included using an unprofessional screen name, being linked to criminal behavior, and sharing confidential information from previous employers.[3] Can you believe?

So now that it's clear that you'll only put your best foot forward on the likes of LinkedIn, how can you help recruiters and hiring managers—who comprise 27 percent of LinkedIn subscribers—as well as prospective clients, find you?[4] Peter Engel, a senior recruiter with Cantor Executive Search Solutions, which specializes in the public relations industry, says that he particularly likes using LinkedIn for getting the most up-to-date information on candidates. He mainly uses keywords (e.g., social media, health care, business to business, crisis communications, writer, agency, broadcast) when searching for candidates.

"LinkedIn helps me connect the dots from prospective candidates to people whose reputations I know of. For example, if I look up a job candidate and see that the person has 50 connections, the chances are pretty good that I'll know 5 percent of them either directly or by reputation. If I see Jane Smith at XYZ Agency on LinkedIn, I might say, 'Oh yeah, I remember her. Is she still there?'

"From there," he continues, "I will reach out to Jane with a specific reason in mind. I will soon know whether Jane is working, looking for a job, or might be attractive for a position I'm looking to fill.

Whether Jane is interested in that particular job or not, I've made contact and added her updated résumé to my database. If she's looking for a job in a few months, she's top of mind. It's a way for everyone to win." LinkedIn is also a useful tool for researching companies and identifying who in your professional network is connected to someone in those companies. Let the introductions begin!

Your Online Social Network

Howard Greenstein, a social media strategist and evangelist, and president of the Harbrooke Group consultancy, talks about how you can use social media to increase your visibility and build your network: "Social networking sites enable you to connect with people you went to college with or worked with in previous jobs. Many can alert you to the presence of people from companies you list in your employment history. These people can see what you've done and when you change your employment status."

He offers an example: "So if you've been promoted from associate to vice president, the site will alert your network, and people can get in touch. This can help build your prominence in your career. Another nice feature is that as you build your network, you can send questions to your contacts. And when people in your network pose questions, you can answer them. If your answers are well regarded, people can rate them. The more people who rate you on providing answers on a particular topic, the more likely you'll get a little badge that says you're an expert." Greenstein describes more of the potential benefits: "So it can actually bring you accolades just by participating in this kind of conversation. You can also find jobs and opportunities on these sites."

Advice for Newcomers to Social Media

Greenstein offers advice to social media newcomers: "First, try out some of the social networks with a few trusted people—maybe a techie or a frequent user. Ask them to invite you into their online networks. That way, you can build up your network slowly and get used to the site. Read the help section. Many of these sites have a blog where you can learn what the leaders of the company are thinking about and what features they're adding."

As much as I love the unlimited potential of the Web, I have mixed feelings about some aspects of social networking. The main reason I'm not more active on social networking sites is that I'm private by nature and not comfortable with, in effect, sharing the names of my contacts with anyone who cares to inquire. So if someone I know invites me to join her network, I usually agree. However, I don't actively invite people to join my network—and certainly not my coaching clients, many of whom don't want it to be known that they're working with a coach. You may have similar concerns or you may just want to expand your network through other Internet options, such as blogs and podcasts, both of which we'll discuss now with Greenstein.

Blogs

"I marvel at how blogs have completely shifted the landscape of how everyone from sole proprietors to news media to major corporations can communicate with their constituents in a more informal and timely way," says Greenstein. "The important part of a blog is the ability for readers to leave comments in an interactive format. That back-and-forth communication builds the blog community." He continues: "Blogs also let other Web sites—especially search engines—know when new content is available. So when you publish a new blog entry, most blog software will send off a little 'ping' notice to Google, Yahoo!, and other big search engines to say: 'Hey, there's new content here.' Usually in 10 to 15 minutes your new content is indexed and available to people searching for it. It's an opportunity for you to share your opinions and create a human presence, especially if you're a small to mid-sized business."

Adds Senia Maymin, publisher and editor in chief of the daily news site PositivePsychologyNews.com: "Of our 30 plus authors, at least a quarter have their own blogs and newsletters. The best thing for an introvert about running a blog is that it's interaction on your own terms, on your own time, and it doesn't feel pressured by the readers. You set the agenda. You can decide what time of day you want to interact." (I like that we can now all be citizen journalists. The downside of the blogosphere is the unevenness of quality out there. However, that varies in traditional media as well.)

Greenstein talks about how you can benefit by creating your own blog: "Publishing a blog can help you build your business by telling people what you care about, how you do business, your customer service philosophy, anecdotes of how you've served customers, and products that you recommend. Also, most people who run a business have a Web site that's static, like a brochure. Since it doesn't change often, there's little reason for people to come back after they've seen it once. In contrast, blog content can change constantly." Greenstein mentions some useful resources: "Books I recommend on blogging include *Naked Conversations* by Robert Scoble and Shel Israel and *Now Is Gone* by Geoff Livingston and Brian Solis."

Podcasts

If you'd rather speak than write, podcasts are a simple way for you to get out your message. In case you've heard of podcasts but still aren't sure exactly what they are, here's how Greenstein describes them: "A podcast is a digital media file distributed over the Internet for playback on a portable media player or a personal computer." He adds: "It's effectively a radio program on the Net made by an amateur or a pro. The difference between a podcast and an audio download is that you can subscribe to a podcast, and every time it's updated, it can appear on your computer or in your media player. Like a magazine, 'subscriptions' is the word we use, but typically, there is no cost to get a podcast.

"Audio podcasts can sound pretty professional with just a $70 microphone setup," notes Greenstein. "Lots of services will host your podcast for free. They often put an advertisement at the beginning or the end of your podcast as the quid pro quo trade-off. There are also other services that will host your podcasts for a fixed monthly amount. Blog Talk Radio lets you do a podcast using only your telephone!" Some self-promoters go a step further by grabbing their video cameras and posting their videos to YouTube. "But," Greenstein warns, "videocasts aren't so easy to create. They can look amateurish and unprofessional if they're not well considered." He continues: "To learn more about podcasting, attend Podcamp events, which are free or inexpensive conferences held all over the world (www.podcamp.org), or read *Tricks of the Podcasting Masters* by Rob Walsh and Mur Lafferty."

Our ability to go inward and concentrate before we take action is one of the gifts that we often take for granted as introverts. In this chapter you picked your self-promotion goals, you created a marketing mix of the activities you handpicked to get you there, and you either built or considered (if you're not much of a planner) a personalized game plan that makes the best use of your time and money. So now, rather than sending you out on "Mission: Impossible," you're well equipped with the tools to build your empire (or just make a few calls).

Which leads us to Chapter 4. Imagine someone trying to sell you the best prime rib on the planet—and you're a vegetarian. Or pressuring you to join the local parent-teachers association—and you don't have kids. Self-promoting or selling always involves at least two parties—for simplicity, let's call them a buyer and a seller. You can save yourself so much scrambling and guesswork by learning about your target audiences, or the people who are most likely to be a match for your offerings. As always, we'll go inward to see what you can learn using your quiet strengths. I hope you enjoy the discovery process. Ready?

REFLECTIONS AND ACTIONS

What You Learned

1. _____

_____

2. _____

_____

3. _____

_____

Action: What will you do?	How You'll Do It: What support or further information will you obtain?	Accountability: Whom will you tell about this action?	Completion Date: By when?

four

Your Target Audiences

Going Inward and Reaching Outward

Your target audiences have needs and wants, and you have plenty to offer. In this chapter we'll look at the overlap between what they want and what you've got. Your target audiences are anyone you want to reach: your boss, your colleagues, your clients and prospects, your mentors, people who can recommend you or connect you to opportunities, those who read your blog, and so on. While it may sound daunting to appeal to all these stakeholders, you can do so well by using your introvert's propensities for researching, quietly analyzing ways to reach them, offering expertise they will value, writing information that will interest them, and building deep, lasting relationships with them.

You already have extensive experience as a target audience—for everything from life insurance to car repairs. People are trying to sell you stuff every day, and you can't possibly buy it all. What makes you buy what you buy? Chances are you go for what you need or want. Simply put, you'll buy whatever answers the question that advertisers broadcast on the fictional yet popular commercial-only radio station What's In It For Me?—or WIIFM. It's not a new concept, and it's basic, yet it's easy to forget. So I'll remind you of it periodically.

Before we go further into the heads of those you'll target, we'll look at what goes through *your* head when someone tries to sell you something or promote herself to you. Not to say that your target audience necessarily thinks the way you do; however, this can be a useful starting point. Along the same lines, in this chapter we'll explore your hiring decisions to gain insights about why people would hire you. Ultimately, you'll find a way of promoting yourself that honors both you and your target audiences. No need to do anything embarrassing or beneath you. Much of what we'll cover in this chapter overlaps with the chapters on networking, public speaking, and interviewing. However, here we'll zero in on targeting your audiences, which is essential to your success at all of those self-promotion activities.

YOU, YOU, YOU

I have a mantra to help you whenever you think of promoting yourself: You, you, you. Certainly, when I'm on the buying side of the equation and the seller makes everything about me, me, me, my WIIFM kicks in and the seller can engage me with minimal effort. And so it follows that when I'm the one wearing the seller's hat, my mantra reminds me to focus on my target audience—to ultimately reach them, them, them.

This mantra affects the way I do business, even in small ways. For example, I usually start e-mails and phone conversations with a line or two about the other person—inquiring about her latest news, congratulating him on his promotion, or referring to our last exchange. I get to why I'm touching base quickly—but not without first showing interest in the other person. Starting with an open-ended question (hint: they often start with *who, what, where, when, why,* or *how*) is particularly helpful for us introverts because it gets our conversation partners talking while we take our time warming up. What mantra can remind you whom to focus on when you're promoting yourself?

PITCHING AND RECEIVING PITCHES

While I certainly wasn't born to sell (anything, including myself), I often find being sold to even more unwelcome. Even though I know better on a conscious level, when I think of selling or being sold to, the first few words that come to my introverted mind are: *invading*, *pushing*, and *stretching the truth*. Clearly, I'm not alone in my bias: Development Dimensions International (DDI), a global talent management consultancy, found that 46 percent of corporate buyers surveyed across six countries (Australia, Canada, France, Germany, the United Kingdom, and the United States) said that they would not be proud to call themselves salespeople. The buyers most commonly described their perceptions of the sales process as "a necessary evil." Worse, colorful descriptions they used to describe salespeople included "irritating, like a rash you want to scratch but your doctor won't let you," "leeches," and "they come, they lie, they steal, they go."[1] Do you have biases about salespeople that make you leery about selling? If you see salespeople as slick or condescending purveyors of useless products who sneer at your questions, then how do you justify selling—including selling yourself—without feeling like a phony?

A client of mine we'll call Maria Maldonado, an international banker and specialist in Latin American economic affairs, offers her insights about the different ways that introverts and extroverts approach selling. "I've seen two kinds of selling," she says. "One kind is the banker who builds relationships that deepen in time. People who are more introverted do well with these one-on-one encounters. The other is the product people that the banker calls in to ask, for example: 'Can you sell Treasury or foreign exchange services to this client?' The product salespeople parachute in, give a presentation to sell their product, and parachute out." She points out: "That's much harder for an introvert because it doesn't entail relationship building."

Maldonado goes on to say, "If you're more introverted, selling is much easier when you have passion. I always believe in what I'm selling and give a lot of thought about the impact of my banking products on my clients. I get clear about the specifics of how I can help them, and that helps convince them. When you gain good clients, they give you business, you get more opportunities, and you gain visibility in your industry. That helps you to the next step." She concludes with an encouraging reminder: "One success builds on the other."

You don't have to make grand gestures or launch major media campaigns to effectively target your audiences. Sometimes, small, memorable actions are all it takes. Think of the last time someone promoted herself successfully to you. Chances are you felt engaged rather than bamboozled because the self-promoter solved a problem, addressed a need, provided you a shortcut, or otherwise delivered something that you were interested in. She listened to you and helped you to visualize a solution. You were so absorbed that you might not have even noticed that she was trying to sell you something. In effect, you were on the same side of the table.

How Google Stepped into the Shoes of Its Target Audience

More than 10 years ago, Web sites with flashy banner ads proliferated on the Web. Many went bust because Web advertising wasn't that effective. Then Google came along and offered a top-notch search capability coupled with a simple but brilliant idea—that when people are searching for something, they may also be interested in buying items related to it. Google sold simple text ads with no flash and became immediately profitable. The brains at Google put themselves in the shoes of their target audience and delivered what people who conduct searches wanted. The rest is history.

YOU AND YOUR TARGET AUDIENCES

Now let's talk about your target audiences, or the people who need or want what you have to offer. It may come as a relief to realize that they're probably only a tiny sliver of the population, rather than "el mundo." The clearer you are about who is in that sliver and what you can offer that they'll care about, the better you can target them. Gaining this clarity can help you focus your efforts, rather than waste your energy—a precious resource for an introvert—trying to please everyone. Envision yourself as a problem solver for a specific segment of the population, rather than as a glad-handing lounge lizard.

Let's do an exercise to help you think further about your target audience. You can write in the target audiences you identified in Chapter 3 or other people, groups, or organizations you'd like to target in the left-hand column in the table that follows. You may not have all the information you need at this point; however, take a stab at it and see what you currently know as well as what you'll need to find out.

In case you still need to be convinced that connecting with your target audiences is important, picture throwing darts without a bull's-eye to target. You point with no aim, you throw, and your dart lands anywhere. How do you know if you've succeeded if you don't know what you're targeting? If instead you aim at a bull's-eye, you'll know exactly when you've hit the mark.

Take it from Steve Orr, MarketWatch Radio Network anchor: "People pitch us stories, and it drives me crazy when they have no idea what we do. I'll ask them: 'Do you realize we're a business radio network?' There's nothing worse than a PR person's calling us with a story that has nothing to do with what we cover."

Targeting your audiences is not as much an exact science as it is considering an aggregate of many variables, including their needs, moods, cultural background, financial status, personal chemistry,

What You Can Offer Your Target Audiences

Your Target Audience (Write the names of individuals, groups, or organizations in the lines below.)	What Problem You Can Help Them Solve (i.e., Their WIIFM)	Why You're Qualified to Help Them	The Best Time to Reach Them	The Best Way to Reach Them (e.g., E-mail, Text Message, Phone, Letter, through a Mutual Acquaintance)	Who You Know in Common (i.e., for a Possible Introduction)	How Often You Can Reach Them (e.g., Daily Blog, Monthly Newsletter, Holiday Card)

Life after the White House

"I was walking my dog, Charlie, and I passed a restaurant with the doors open so I could see inside," says author-actor Laurie Graff. "There was a man sitting front and center, facing the outside. I said, 'Oh, my God, that's Bill Clinton." She continues: "My book (*Looking for Mr. Goodfrog*) had come out two weeks earlier with a little section in it about Bill. I flew with Charlie back to my apartment, screaming to my mother on my cell phone, 'I'm going to give Clinton a book!' We both love him. I grabbed one of my books, ran back to the restaurant, asked a busboy to watch Charlie, and said to a waiter while pointing at Clinton: 'I just need to give him something. I'll be a second.' Clinton looked up with those beautiful blue eyes, and I said, 'Excuse me, I don't mean to interrupt, but I wrote this book and it just came out and I want you to have it and you're in it.' I went to walk away when he said, 'It's a funny thing, because I happen to love frogs. I collect them. Not real ones. Figurines. I have about 200 at home.' Then we got to talking. I told him how much I missed him as president. I said I thought Chelsea would like this book. Clinton said he would read it. Six months later I sent him a copy of my prior book (*You Have to Kiss a Lot of Frogs*) with a letter thanking him for his kindness the night we met. He wrote back and thanked me. He makes people feel like they count."

So, how did Graff target her audience? She took a risk, seized the moment, and offered a gift—a book she had just written that has glowing references to Clinton. She could have assumed that Clinton, given his high profile and how much he's been written about, wouldn't be interested. Instead, she took a chance, risked rejection, and just went for it. She emanated confidence in her book and showed genuine warmth and enthusiasm toward Clinton.

How did Graff promote herself? If Clinton says a good word about the book to anyone, what an endorsement! How did Clinton promote himself, in turn? He connected on a human level and lived up to his reputation of making Graff feel as if she were the only person in the room. I'm sure she didn't make that a secret to her vast network!

timing, and so much more. If that sounds overwhelming, keep in mind your advantages as an introvert. You're more inclined to learn as much as you can about your audiences and think deeply about how you can make a difference to them. "Take the pulse of the situation and listen to what your animal instincts are telling you," says Marianna Lead, Ph.D., founder of Goal Imagery® Institute. "You'll see that it's not about you, and it's not about them. Instead, it's about a new entity: *you-them*." She continues: "How intimate, truthful, and real you want this relationship to be depends on how intimate, truthful, and real you are willing to be within that moment."

Look at the line-up of people and/or organizations you've identified as targets in the preceding table. What do they have in common? Are they mostly single urban women in their thirties or retired suburban men in their sixties? Do most of them have advanced degrees? Are they demographically diverse, yet all tend to be highly competitive? Also consider sociological factors and other preferences, such as religion, affiliations, and hobbies, that they have in common. It's okay if you don't see any patterns. However, the more you can identify what they have in common, the more you can steer your self-promotion in the right direction.

COLLABORATING WITH YOUR TARGET AUDIENCE

The owner of a consulting firm—let's call him Francis Kelly—contacted me because he needed a coach to help him prepare for a major presentation. Despite his self-confidence and career success, he was terrified of speaking to large audiences. He said he wanted to find a coach in Connecticut because he preferred not to travel to New York City, where I'm based.

When I asked Kelly to envision how a coach could best help him, he described the type of support he needed with planning and rehearsing for a major upcoming presentation. I could have given him a few names of public speaking coaches in Connecticut. However, since I felt a strong connection with him, believed that

I could help him immensely, and didn't mind the 45-minute train ride to his office in Connecticut, I told Kelly I'd like to work with him. He signed up.

My conversation with Kelly was a collaboration rather than a sales pitch. I promoted myself successfully to this prospective client by asking him to describe his goals for coaching, and together we created a game plan. I could have taken Kelly's request for a coach in Connecticut on face value, referred him to another coach, and moved on. However, by asking questions and learning more, I found a valued new client, and he found the support he needed to make an outstanding presentation—a mutual win.

So it can be useful to delve into a prospective client's needs to determine how we can best help him. How do you get beneath the surface and discover his actual needs and wants? Tap into your introverted inclinations to listen and think deeply, and then find ways to be helpful. None of this should feel as though you're pushing. The more we can get to know our prospective clients and employers on a human level and find out what matters to them, the better we are at promoting ourselves to them.

Be clear about what you can offer members of your target audiences—whether they're actual decision makers who can hire you or people who influence them. While it may also be appropriate to say what you *can't* offer, lead with the positive. Describe what you *can* do, rather than starting with the hard truths about how you can't make all their dreams come true.

GAINING MUTUAL BENEFIT

When we promote ourselves to someone successfully, the result is often that both parties benefit. In the case of Kelly and me, he got a coach to help him overcome a major stumbling block in his career and I got a new client whom I was delighted to work with. I never had to "sell" Kelly on my services. All I did was listen actively and ask open-ended questions; ultimately, we found a solution together that benefited both of us.

PROMOTING YOURSELF TO SOMEONE MORE SENIOR

Do you find it more challenging to promote yourself to someone more senior, or advanced in her career, than you? While doing so can be intimidating, keep in mind the benefits that the senior manager stands to gain from learning what you have to offer. For example, you could potentially fill a staffing need for the senior manager. You might even reinforce her networking clout when she gets to call a colleague to offer a match for his organization (e.g., you or someone in your network).

Organizations don't typically hire people as a favor. More likely they hire because they have a need to fill and they're looking for results. So articulate the results that you can offer. There's also something to be said for allowing someone to be generous toward you and then showing your appreciation. Then, when the time comes, you can find ways to be helpful in turn—by doing something the other person will value, such as sharing knowledge and making introductions.

WHY YOU HIRE PEOPLE

Businesses don't hire people. People hire people. When I reflect on my own hiring decisions, I realize that personal connection plays a big role. Gary Osland, account director at mNovakDesign, agrees: "If I have a choice between two people to do a job, my criteria are: 'First, can they actually execute?'" he says. "The next is: 'Do I trust them?' And the third, if everything is equal: 'Who do I like best?'"

When you're in a position to hire, what makes you pick one candidate over another? Why do you choose a particular dentist, hairdresser, babysitter, or staff member at work over another equally qualified one? Is trust the most important criterion when you hire an accountant and a sense of aesthetics when you choose an interior decorator? Or do you have different priorities? Think about what has influenced you to pick the people you have picked. Has it been their passion for their subject matter? Their connection to you? The level of confidence they've inspired in you? Cost? Convenience? Something else? This thinking process will help you step outside yourself and ultimately gain insight about why someone would hire you.

WHY PEOPLE HIRE YOU

Using your reasons for hiring others as a backdrop for the following exercise, now let's look at why people hire you. It's easy to make assumptions. The real answers can be elusive. So let's consider why someone would hire you or contract your services—beyond the nuts-and-bolts job requirements that so many candidates meet.

Use your introverted abilities to go inward and think deeply to begin to find your answers. Think about what you wrote in the preceding table titled What You Can Offer Your Target Audiences. How much overlap is there between what you can offer and what your target audiences have appreciated about you in the past? What do they value overall? After you've gone inward, this might be a good time to do a little market research to learn more. If it's appropriate, ask trusted bosses, clients, and even managers at places where you've done volunteer work throughout your career specifically why they've chosen to work with you. You may be surprised by their answers.

Assuming that you and the other candidates have comparable levels of experience and expertise, note in the grid that follows the top reasons you think people have hired you or contracted your services. First write the name of one of your managers or clients at the top of each column. Then write a 1 for the reason you think was most important to each target audience, 2 for the next most important one, and so on. Of course, if you do ask these stakeholders, add in the actual reasons they give you.

Reasons People Have Hired You

Reasons	Target Audience 1 Name:	Target Audience 2 Name:	Target Audience 3 Name:
Trust			
Convenience			
Your fee and/or compensation level			
Your passion			
Comfort			
Confidence			
Thoroughness			
Prominence in field			
Warmth			
Family and/or friend connection			
Reliability			
Freebies you offer			
Efficiency			
Your office space			
Your office staff			
Other:			

Many of my clients have shared that their human connection with the hiring manager was pivotal in their getting the job, assuming that their qualifications were on a par with those of the other candidates. This realization has helped them focus on the importance of building relationships, rather than wasting energy trying to "sell" themselves or overemphasize their qualifications.

WHAT YOU TAKE FOR GRANTED ABOUT YOURSELF

After completing the Reasons People Have Hired You exercise—especially if you actually asked others why they hired you—you may have found that some of the main reasons your bosses and clients have had for hiring you are qualities you take for granted about yourself. These may include some of your most stellar qualities, yet you haven't noticed them because they come easily to you or they've always been there. Still, these qualities may be what others most appreciate about you.

In the space that follows, name three of your qualities that you take for granted at least some of the time. Mine are these: (1) I can often hear the subtext, or what's not being said, in a conversation. (2) I have a high level of compassion. And (3) I'm adept at creating orderly systems out of chaos. Do I remind myself of those traits every day? Well, it wouldn't kill me, especially if these are qualities my target audiences value. It's important that I'm at least aware of these qualities.

What do you take for granted about yourself? List three of your assets that you sometimes forget about in the space that follows. It might help to refer back to the responses you received when you informally surveyed your dream team regarding what they appreciate about you in Chapter 1. It might help to do a little market research here too and to get input from a confidante or two.

1. _____

_____

2. _____

_____

3. _____

_____

What insights have you had by thinking about what you take for granted about yourself? From my experience, the clearer you are about your assets, the clearer others will be. How can becoming more aware of what you take for granted about yourself help you in targeting your audiences? It's back to the definition we started with at the beginning of this chapter. To effectively target your audiences, look at the overlap between what they want and what you've got. You have a lot of attributes. Which ones do your target audiences value most?

QUALITY CONNECTIONS

Anne Houle, senior manager for leadership training at Saks Fifth Avenue, has this closing advice on the value of targeting people who seem right for you: "Quality connections, not quantity, are especially important for an introvert. Cultivate one-on-one relationships, and believe your gut as to whom you can trust."

To exemplify Houle's point, one of my target audiences is made up of introverts who hire me to coach them on their self-promotion efforts. These clients have all made a commitment to work on something essential to them and have entrusted me as their thinking partner and stalwart supporter. Whether I work with them for six weeks or a year, the relationships often become deep, and we can forever become a part of one another's professional networks. These clients are also a source of referral business. For all these reasons, I strongly value and nurture those relationships. How does this apply to you? Target people who are a good match for you, who will become welcome additions to your network, and who won't drain your energy.

Now that you've identified your target audiences and explored what they value in you, in the next chapter you'll go outward to meet them and learn how to apply more of your introvert's advantages to further boost your buzz.

REFLECTIONS AND ACTIONS

What You Learned

1. _____

_____

2. _____

_____

3. _____

_____

Action: What will you do?	How You'll Do It: What support or further information will you obtain?	Accountability: Whom will you tell about this action?	Completion Date: By when?

five

Your Network

Expanding Your Sphere of Influence

This story is real. Some details have been changed because . . . well, it's a small world. "It was a bloodbath," whispers a Chanel-clad HR executive whom we'll call Ginger Parker. "They canned my boss and put my nemesis in charge of the department. I called in sick the next day and made a list of everyone I could possibly contact," she says. "It was red-alert time. I had to get the hell out."

Parker, who is an introvert, shares how she got into gear: "I brainstormed names of everyone I could think of—friends, family, former bosses, clients, colleagues, people from elevators, shoe stores, Jacuzzis, and bat mitzvahs." She reflects: "Thankfully, over the years, I had always been generous about connecting people, sharing information, leads, staying in touch, and offering my talents as a problem solver.

"I didn't realize how many people would be happy to help me," Parker continues. "The outpouring of support was phenomenal and landed me my next job within a few months in an unexpected way. An acquaintance I had met bungee jumping in New Zealand a year earlier offered to introduce me to a colleague. The acquaintance was a bond trader. I was a senior human resources manager—different worlds—but within a few weeks, I got a sizzling hot offer at a competitor, and packed my bags and never looked back."

Parker's story demonstrates the value of networking, which we'll define as building business relationships for mutual benefit. Networking works best as a lifelong pursuit rather than as self-promotion CPR when you need a job or want to power up your business during down times. "I treasure that I have a lot of people in my network and that I can help make connections," says Gary Osland, account director at mNovakDesign. "No matter what my colleagues are looking for—whether it's a good speech writer, chiropractor, or a locksmith—they come to me. I value that they put trust in my recommendations." He adds: "And the goodwill usually comes back to me."

> The world would be a much better place if everybody knew one great stunt, magic trick, or practical joke to pull on their friends.
> —**Mac King, comedy magician, Las Vegas**

As an introvert, you'd probably rather listen than talk most of the time. You're adept at building deep and lasting relationships. You're trusted, accountable, and a core contributor. People look to you for your expertise. However, you're not a schmoozer. You value your space and quiet time. Regardless, you have distinct advantages that enable you to create a strong network that can provide you with continuous support.

Why network? A CareerXroads study of name-brand firms' use of networking found that the number 1 external source of new hires was referrals (28 percent), while the second largest source was online job boards (26 percent).[1] So from the standpoint of hiring organizations, word of mouth is the best way to find you. Likewise, if you're an independent consultant or business owner, your network—including the clients and colleagues who sing your praises—is probably what pays your bills. So how are prospective clients and employers going to find you unless you tell people in your network that you're for hire?

In this chapter we'll talk about how you can apply your existing gifts and resources to strengthening your professional network. However, before you make your first phone call, identify what you can offer, who will be interested, what's in it for the other party, and what you want from your network. We'll cover getting recognition for your expertise; intercultural aspects of self-promotion; the ways you spend your networking time; and your sphere of influence—that is, who you know; how to ask for help; how to have informational interviews, which can help you expand and deepen your network; and how to break the ice in social situations. We'll also discuss your elevator pitch, or the all-important answer to: "So tell me about yourself"; how to handle business cards; and how to present yourself with confidence. All you need to get started is a computer, a phone, and a smile. Ready?

POSITION YOURSELF AS A VALUED EXPERT

Shoya Zichy, author (with Ann Bidou) of *Career Match*, offers you advice that will help you raise your visibility: "Join organizations, volunteer your time, and take on special initiatives within your company." She adds: "Find projects in which you can work with people from other departments, and be generous with your expertise. Also, write for company and industry publications whenever possible." Zichy emphasizes the benefit of this approach for introverts: "Rather than being known for your charm, you become known as an expert providing a valuable service."

Zichy gives the example of the former CEO of a Fortune 500 company she knows who is deeply introverted. Her contact was aware that he needed additional visibility, but he just wasn't the type to schmooze in clubs in the Hamptons. Instead, as an art expert, he joined the board of a major museum. "That's a big reason why all these people serve on volunteer boards," says Zichy. "It's often because of who will be sitting next to them." Volunteering on a board will allow you to interact regularly, possibly over the course of a year or more, with others who share a common interest with you. This will give you ample opportunities to form deep, lasting relationships with a select few of your fellow volunteer board members. Perfect for an introvert.

Getting Guidance

We have an organization at Baruch College called Executives on Campus, which brings executives and working professional people to the campus to mentor, coach, and guide the students. It enables the students to network with peers across industries. I can't tell you how many people have made career changes or job changes through the connections they made at EOC.

—**Kathleen Waldron, Ph.D., president of Baruch College**

NETWORKING IN THE SPIRIT OF SHARING

You can reframe self-promotion as a more palatable activity by approaching it as a way of connecting and sharing with people you would enjoy knowing. One of my clients went out of his way to help three of his colleagues this week. He didn't ask for anything in exchange—and he didn't need to. A gifted but unassuming introvert, my client helped his colleagues because he enjoys connecting talented people with attractive opportunities. The generosity usually comes back to him, often in spades, and often when he's least expecting it. He doesn't push or pressure anyone. Of course, not everyone subscribes to the spirit of sharing. However, my client surrounds himself with people who understand the value of relationships and who look out for their colleagues over time.

So you're a lawyer who addresses the needs of someone who has been wronged and is entitled to justice. You're a technical writer who can translate complex concepts into plain English. Conveying these gifts is not just self-promotion—it's letting others know that you have what they need. Kathleen Waldron, Ph.D., president of Baruch College, suggests a forum to help you spread the word: "You could cohost a lunch," she says. "You bring people together, and they can have an interesting conversation. You show your leadership that way, and it doesn't demand that you're the public speaker or that you put yourself out there, which you may not be comfortable doing if you're really introverted."

DON'T TAKE ANYTHING PERSONALLY

Of course, some people will respond to your efforts to connect and others won't. "Don't take things personally," says Max Victor Alper, Ph.D., a fine art photographer who exhibits widely throughout the United States and Europe. I've heard this advice before, and it's easier said than done. Here's Alper's approach: "As an artist, I have developed a dual consciousness—one that is aesthetic/spiritual, and the other in tune with the real/material world. This awareness protects me from the negativity of other people. When creating, an artist exists in a zone of beauty and truth that is akin to a spiritual experience. The creative process is exhilarating, while real life frequently seems diminished." He concludes with a reflection that's at once grounded and expansive: "So I feel like a religious zealot who will not permit other people's criticism to destroy my faith in this extraordinary realm of creativity."

Let's bring our attention back to the real/material world. My general rule when it comes to networking is this: Three tries and I'm out. If you're a prospective client and you show interest in hearing from me, it's our mutual loss if you don't respond to my phone messages and e-mails. You don't get the benefit of what I have to offer, and I don't get the benefit of working with you. Will I let it ruin my weekend when you don't call me back? I doubt it. You may have gotten into a bubbly stew all of a sudden at work, you may have had to leave town, or you may just be a flake. I don't care. My time is valuable too. Besides, I have to get back to my own beauty and truth!

So what can we take away from all of this? When you invest your time and energy to connect with someone and you don't hear back after persisting several times, free yourself up to pursue other opportunities. It beats getting sucked into the vortex of self-doubt that many of us introverts are prone to. While it's important to be aware of how you approach others, it can be self-defeating to second-guess yourself and ascribe your contacts' unresponsiveness to something you did wrong.

INTERCULTURAL ASPECTS OF SELF-PROMOTION

I met Shakti Gattegno at Teachers College, Columbia University, where she was conducting a workshop for language teachers that I attended. At a later point, I mentioned this book to her, and we discussed the idea of including a section on the intercultural aspects of self-promotion. I told her that the topic was so big that I was concerned I couldn't do it justice in just a few paragraphs. Gattegno, who was born in India and has lived in England, Switzerland, and the United States, responded by sharing with me a rhetorical question she had heard as a child: "How is it that the sun is so big, and yet a small umbrella can cover it?" She added that the topic of intercultural self-promotion was indeed profound and big, yet we could begin to cover it. And those who want to can seek out a lot more. So here goes.

Some of my clients from around the world find it distasteful—if not repugnant—to talk about their accomplishments. While plenty of my U.S.-born clients are just as reluctant to promote themselves, those from other countries and cultures face other layers of challenges. Many of my international clients didn't grow up having to constantly promote themselves. They already navigate multiple intercultural and language issues in the United States on a daily basis, and so adding self-promotion to the mix can seem daunting—especially for introverts.

Gattegno says that when she is communicating with people from other cultures, she finds it most important to be mindful of their *humanness*. She emphasizes the importance of *transcending* while not rejecting one's own culture and appreciating the cultures of others. Adds Vincent Suppa, head of The Middle Way One World Company®: "How do we preserve the humility that's part of our cultural heritage and still promote our accomplishments?" He answers: "By making self-promotion less about you and more about the people you serve."

"When I promote myself," Suppa says, "it's ultimately about promoting my customers, my vendors, and everyone else who makes our sustainable venture succeed every day." Middle Way helps indigenous farmers in Asia sell their plant extracts to U.S.-based companies committed to sustainable development, such as Aveda. He continues: "So if you helped save a company from bankruptcy, tell the story of working families that depended on their jobs, the customers they served, and how much it meant to all of you that your company became solvent. Audiences have a tremendous capacity to hear what is *not* directly thrown in their face." He adds: "Follow this advice and both your self-promotion and humanity will remain intact."

Simi Sanni Nwogugu, CEO of HOD Consulting, Inc., a diversity consulting organization, offers the following advice to culturally diverse introverts inside organizations: "Take time to study the environment and carefully select one person, or a few people, you admire most—preferably in senior management. Seek them out and cultivate strategic one-on-one mentoring relationships with them." Nwogugu, who divides her time between New York and her native city of Lagos, Nigeria, makes a good point: "Make sure you contribute to their learning as much as you want them to contribute to yours. Tell them the things you're working on that excite you. Your positive energy will energize them, and when an opportunity comes up for a promotion or a special project requiring the specific skills and competencies you've communicated your passion around, they will tell you about it first." She adds: "In everything, be authentic—know yourself and what you want. Don't measure yourself by someone else's yardstick."

INTERCULTURAL TIPS

While it's impossible to address the full range of challenges that people from each country and culture face when they promote themselves in the United States, I've compiled a list of tips to get you started. Even if you grew up in the United States, you may find that your work environment has its own distinct culture that feels like a different planet. In fact, the corporate world, with its hierarchies and unwritten and sometimes intransigent rules, can seem that way to many. So you may glean some useful insights, regardless of where you're from.

- **Take credit when it's due to you.**   Although this may be one of the most challenging aspects of promoting yourself as an introvert, attach your name to your ideas, contributions, and accomplishments. Take ownership of them at meetings, get on the agenda to enhance your visibility, and include your name on whatever you write.
- **Just state the facts when you talk about your accomplishments.**   Use your introvert's inclination to think deeply about how you want to position yourself. The more concrete the details and data and the fewer the adjectives, the better. For example: "My product development efforts have contributed to a 25 percent increase in revenues this year." Practice saying it.
- **Ask colleagues, managers, clients, and other people you know to introduce you to people you want to meet and to refer business to you.**   This is one of the best ways for an introvert to expand her network, increase her clout, and gain more access. The introductions can be in person, but they can also be by phone or e-mail.
- **Create and practice an elevator pitch out loud.**   The concept of having a few crisp sentences already crafted to present yourself and what you do may be new to you. See the section titled "So Tell Me about Yourself" later in this chapter to learn more.

- **Tell a story.** People remember stories. They're an excellent way to find common ground across cultures. "I've made presentations all over the United States, but more importantly in Europe and Asia," says Doug Fidoten, president of Dentsu America, Inc., a full-service advertising and marketing-communications company. "I've done presentations that were simultaneously translated into Chinese and Japanese, with people from Europe in the same audience. Even though we're in the business world and our presentations have to be concise, when I get up and address a group, I need to tell a story."

- **Use self-deprecating humor.** "Laughing at oneself doesn't offend anyone, is culturally safe, and is central to making you more accessible," says Vincent Suppa. Be particularly mindful that any self-deprecating humor you use is also self-respecting. While it's fine to laugh at yourself in a gentle and charming manner, you risk losing your audience's respect if you put yourself down harshly. "If humor is at the heart of a memorable presentation, self-deprecating humor is the humanity behind the humor," Suppa adds.

HOW YOU SPEND YOUR NETWORKING TIME

Let's look at how you spend your networking time today versus your ideal. For the exercise in the box that follows, use these simple instructions, and start by first focusing on the circle to the left, labeled "Actual":

1. Pencil in how many hours (or minutes!) per week, on average, you spend networking to support your professional goals.
2. Slice up the circle—like a pizza—with each slice proportionately representing your networking activities (e.g., reconnecting with past colleagues by phone, e-mail, letter, or blog; making cold calls; following up on leads; attending conferences; writing to people you read about in the press;

attending professional organization meetings; or going to social events).

3. Write each activity in a slice of the pie. Then write down how many hours per week you typically spend engaged in each activity. You may be surprised by this snapshot of how you spend your networking time, which may be more limited for us as introverts.

Before you go on to the circle labeled "Ideal," determine how many hours you can realistically spend on networking, given the way you're wired as an introvert. Consider your preference to think before you speak and your need for more down time between social encounters. For example, after interacting with people at work all day, how much time are you able to spend on networking activities without overly taxing your energy? Now pencil in a realistic number of networking hours above the Ideal Circle. Repeat steps 1 to 3 that you completed for the Actual Circle, but this time, apply them to the Ideal Circle. One of my clients asked if quiet promotional activities, such as e-mailing his contacts to request informational interviews, counted as networking time. Sure, that's part of the mix.

Your Networking Time per Week	
Actual	**Ideal**
I spend ___ hours per week networking.	Ideally, I could spend ___ hours per week networking.

ACTION STEPS

Take a moment to reflect on how you currently spend your networking time and, ideally, how you would apportion the time differently. Then, in the space that follows, list three actions you'll take to further your networking efforts, and commit to a deadline for each. Make the actions concrete and specific. If possible, quantify them (e.g., "I'll approach five new people at networking events this month; I'll follow up by e-mail within 24 hours with those with whom I feel a sufficiently strong connection.").

Your Networking Action Steps	
Action	Deadline
1.	
2.	
3.	

Reflect on your answers. What insights have you had after doing this exercise? Some of my clients have said, for example, that they're actually spending the right amount of time on networking, given their energy levels and all that they're juggling. However, they've added that they would benefit from reallocating their time—spending more of it at events where they're more likely to meet clients and senior managers rather than peers.

YOUR SPHERE OF INFLUENCE

It's time to reflect on whom you've known, currently know, or want to know. Most of my clients find their best opportunities through their professional networks, rather than from ads or headhunters. They know people, introduce them to contacts they'd like to meet, and solve their problems; they also send them invitations, job leads, articles, and holiday cards. My clients get a reputation for their expertise and generosity, and it often comes back around to help them.

Julie Gilbert, who was a senior vice president at Best Buy Co., Inc., at the time of our interview, believes in maintaining a broad and deep network. She says: "You need to build a network outside your company and outside your industry. This enables your work to be much more impactful and better thought out. Your boss will see you doing that, and you can say, 'Hey, I'm going to be on a conference call with Roseanne from GE,' or 'I connected with an individual who's doing research on this subject. Do you want to be on the call with me?' You make it very inclusive. It's just being a smart businessperson." She adds: "Indirectly, you are actually marketing yourself in a way that's really powerful and positive." Gilbert is currently the founder and principal of WOLF (Women's Leadership Forum) Means Business, which, according to its Web site, "reinvents organizations into authentic places where women want to work and that women prefer as customers."

Now that we've talked about how to approach new contacts, let's take stock of whom you already know or could meet through an introduction. In the space that follows (or on a separate sheet of paper if you need more room) write the names of people you know, would like to reconnect with, or would like to meet. Start by writing in the names of the members of your dream team from Chapter 1 and grow it from there.

- ■ Friends:

- ■ Acquaintances:

■ Family members:

■ Neighbors:

■ Colleagues:

■ Managers:

■ Clients:

■ Mentors:

■ People you'd like to meet:

You may be amazed by how many people you know. Keep this list somewhere that is easily accessible, perhaps in a file on your computer. Update it frequently (at least once a quarter), and determine whom you need to contact, when, and for what purpose. Make networking a habit, and get to know people who are further—as well as less far along—in their careers than you are. Find out what each person in your circle is up to and how you can support her or his efforts. This will make asking for help when you need it that much easier. Don't be intimidated by someone's seniority or rank.

While I was writing this book, the U.S. economy slid into a recession, a severe banking crisis hit, the Big Three carmakers were on the brink of bankruptcy, and layoffs were rampant. So many people are dealing with the shock of having to search for a new job without the scaffolding of a strong network that they've invested in over time. Don't let that be you. However, if it is, help is still available—it just may take longer to find the right fit for you in a tight job market.

A quick disclaimer: Some people will ask for lots of help, but they won't be capable of returning (or willing to return) the favor when you need their support. If there's something else you get from the relationship, that's fine. Otherwise, remember that people in your inner circle are there for a reason: they've earned your trust, respect, loyalty, and generosity. Others may just have to wait. . . .

ASKING FOR HELP

You may be generous when people you know need help. I hope so. I find it deeply rewarding to help people in my network get the opportunities they deserve. I make my efforts on their behalf mostly by phone and e-mail, both of which agree with me as an introvert. Since I'm effective as a connector, I know that when I need something, plenty of people will be happy to help me.

Do you know how to ask for help when you need it? It might help to strategize about how to do it, practice your approach, and even get support as you take your first steps. Refer to the names you wrote in the Sphere of Influence exercise, and look at who is likely to root for you. How can you approach them, and what can

Believing in Your Potential

I was raised in the inner city of Philadelphia by a single-parent father; my mother died when I was very young. My father helped us to believe that there was nothing we couldn't do if we worked hard enough. My younger sister became a concert pianist. I graduated from Harvard Law School and went to work at an affluent law firm. I realize every day that I'm only in this position because, pick a year—1963; in that year, the only place in the universe where this was possible was in my father's head. Because he believed it and asserted it over and over again, it became true.

—Ken Frazier, executive vice president and president of
Global Human Health, Merck & Co., Inc.

you ask them to do for you? Whether they can give you feedback on the elevator pitch you're about to craft, introduce you to someone in their organization, or invite you to an event where you can meet your target audience and influencers, it's worth the effort to ask for help.

If you're struggling with what to say, use your introvert's abilities to think deeply about your audience and craft a carefully worded phone script. While there's no need to follow your script word for word, writing down your key points can help you organize your thoughts. You can also use similar wording in a concise e-mail, if that would be a better way to reach your contact. Here's an example of some wording:

> Hi Tina,
> I thought of you the other day while reading about Greenpeace's local efforts—I recall that's an organization you support. It's been a while since we last spoke, and I'd love to know how you're doing. As for me, this is an exciting time because I'm about to change careers. I've always respected your wisdom and experience. Would you be available to meet for coffee in the next few weeks to brainstorm ideas and possibly give me advice about what resources to access and whom to speak with? Perhaps we can meet at the Starbuck's near your office—and, of course, the latte is on me.

A word of caution: One of my clients made his contact list and got ready to stir the pot. He wrote an excellent script and made his first call to an old colleague. She was happy to hear from my client and spent the next hour telling him all about her recent successes. After an hour, my client finally got the message across that he was looking for networking introductions. His colleague asked him if he'd be willing to meet with her niece, who is looking for freelance jobs at organizations like his. My client politely agreed to the request, but when he asked whom the colleague could introduce him to, she changed the subject back to her recent successes. Harrumph.

My client learned to alter his script when calling contacts he knew to be particularly talkative (and not particularly conscious!). He would make his intentions clear up front—first in an e-mail, and then at the beginning of the call. He'd get agreement on how long the call would last and the purpose of the call—for example, "It would be great if we could plan on a half-hour call, at least initially, given how busy we both are. I'd enjoy hearing what you're up to, telling you what I'm pursuing, and exploring whom you might introduce me to for networking purposes. If we need more time, perhaps we could plan on a follow-up call or meet for a drink to catch up. Okay?"

NETWORKING PHONE CALL WORKSHEET

Use the following worksheet to help you organize your networking calls.

- **Objective of call** (Is it to inform, persuade, sell, get action, or build the relationship?):

- **Desired outcome:**

- **Key points:**

- **Target audience—that is, the person you're calling** (What does she or he care about most?):

- **Executive phone presence** (What are you most and least confident about with respect to the call?):

Questions to Help You Prepare

1. What small talk, if any, would be useful to get started—especially if you'll be talking to an extrovert? For example, you might inquire about the other party's recent vacation, ask about someone you know in common, or mention a relevant news item.
2. What are the toughest questions you may be asked, and how will you respond?
3. What is your biggest concern about this call? How can you prepare to address it?
4. What do you need to have near the phone (e.g., water, hard candy, something soothing)?
5. What do you need to do to sound confident (e.g., use vocal variety, speak in your natural pitch, pace yourself)?

Telephone Tips for Introverts

1. Get a phone headset so you can use your phone hands free. This will enable you to take notes more easily.
2. Prepare notes to remind yourself of the most important points you want to get across.
3. Take a few deep breaths before you make the call.
4. Do a quick "sound check" to make sure your voice sounds its best, especially if you're subject to morning-fog voice when you're nervous. Before I pick up the phone, I often say a quick, "Testing: one, two, three," out loud, just to make sure all systems are clear.
5. Audiotape a practice phone call—with or without someone you trust role-playing with you—so you can hear how you come across. Even if you don't feel completely confident, you can still practice sounding that way.
6. Avoid making networking calls from a cell phone. There's nothing like getting your dream contact on the phone only to have cars honking, buses passing, and the call dropped. Also, find a quiet place for your calls.

7. If you're not fluent in English, take extra care to speak slowly, project your voice, and enunciate.
8. Avoid the biggest pitfalls: speaking in a monotone, and allowing your volume to trail off and failing to articulate at the ends of sentences.
9. If you leave a message, say your full name (spell it if necessary), and then clearly state—and repeat—your phone number.

INFORMATIONAL INTERVIEWS

Using many of your strengths as an introvert, you can expand your network exponentially through informational interviews—or brief meetings to build relationships and gain an insider's view into various organizations and industries. Informational interviews can also help open doors for you. As an introvert, you're particularly well suited for informational interviews because you prefer one-on-one interactions to large-group situations. You can go to each meeting prepared, having researched the organization and Googled the person you're meeting with in advance. Listen thoughtfully during the meeting, share your expertise, and follow through with a well-crafted thank you note or e-mail.

While you can approach anyone to request an informational interview, it's often easiest if someone you know—let's call him André Benson—makes an introduction for you in one of three ways:

1. The simplest way is to ask permission to use your contact's name in an introductory e-mail—for example, "André Benson suggested that I contact you."
2. The next approach takes a little more work, but is typically more effective: Ask Benson to introduce you by e-mail, and even send a copy to you. This gives you visibility with the new contact and demonstrates that Benson is vouching for you.

3. The last way is to ask Benson to introduce you in person.
   This can be at an event that the three of you are attending
   or, better yet, at a meeting set up specifically to introduce
   you to Benson's contact.

Here's sample e-mail language that's consistent with the first
scenario I just described:

Subject: André Benson referral

Dear Mr. Pappas:

My colleague André Benson suggested that I contact you.
I'm currently an account executive working on major high-
tech industry accounts at an advertising agency, and I am
exploring the next steps in my career. I'm interested in a
career switch into a business development role in a high-
tech company. Given your experience, I would appreciate
speaking with you briefly— by phone or in person—for
your insights and advice. I will call you at the end of the
week to follow up; if you'd like to reach me in the interim,
I welcome your reply to this e-mail, or you can call me at
212-555-1234.

Regards,
Jay

Jay Schimmel
Account Executive
Phone: 212-555-1234
Fax: 212-555-1235
E-mail: JaySchimmel@xyz.com

Five sentences. That's all you need. Say who referred you (after
getting her or his permission, of course), who you are, and what
you want, and end with a follow-up action. If you don't have a personal connection to the person you're writing to, your approach

can still be similar. You could say how you got the recipient's name (e.g., a trade publication, a blog, an alumni organization, or a job promotion announcement), and your request is the same. The main difference is the outcome.

You're more likely to get a response when you mention the name of someone you both know (even if you just met) or an affiliation you have in common, such as a university or professional organization. Rather than passively waiting for a response to your e-mail, you get another shot by reaching out to the person by phone. Once someone agrees to meet with you, offer to e-mail your questions in advance—as an introvert, you may even enjoy writing them. It demonstrates that you are serious about your search and that you respect the other person's time. Limit the number of questions to just a few, and keep the e-mail succinct.

One more note about e-mails: Use an e-mail address for business that easily identifies you (e.g., MickyGold@xyz.com, and avoid using cute or cryptic e-mail addresses. Ditto emoticons:). Include your full name, title, and contact information (e.g., phone number and e-mail address) at the end of all business e-mails. I can't tell you how many business e-mails I've received that are just signed Cindy. She may have been one of my students, an old colleague, someone I met at a networking event, and so on. Or maybe she's trying to sell me on the deal of a lifetime. You get the point.

Lastly, after you've had your informational interview, send a thank you note. In most cases, I recommend writing it on a high-quality piece of notepaper; however, an e-mail is also fine, particularly if you're writing to a high-tech firm or one located far away (i.e., it would take several days to reach by postal mail). Here's an example of a thank you note:

Dear Tara,

It was great meeting with you today. I enjoyed our conversation about widgets, and particularly about the organizational culture at Widgetco. Thank you for generously offering to introduce me to your colleague, Sandy Smothers.

It sounds as if he and I have a lot in common, given our mutual backgrounds in all stages of widget R&D. I'll keep you posted, and meanwhile, I hope you enjoy the holidays.

Sincerely,
Jo

Jo Milano
Phone: 773-555-2345
E-mail: JoMilano@xyz.com

You may have noticed that I addressed the fictional Pappas more formally, with a courtesy title and his last name, and Tara by her first name. I usually use the Mr. and Ms. greeting in writing when I don't know someone. Once we've met, however, I address people by their first names, unless social protocol (e.g., when writing to people of a certain age, culture, or seniority) or their own preference dictates otherwise.

Janet Riesel, SPHR, an associate director and senior recruiter at Ernst & Young, a Big Four global accounting and financial services firm, adds a few words of caution when sending handwritten or printed thank you notes: "I've noticed that some people—particularly Millennials—use e-mail language. One of my pet peeves are notes that say, 'Hey, Janet,' which is inappropriate." She adds that she often receives thank you notes that are form letters. "I've gotten, 'Thank you for the interview at PricewaterhouseCoopers.' Candidates forget to change the name of the company! They really, really need to check their thank you notes for misspellings and other errors. Even spell check is not sufficient; have someone proofread your work because you will not see your own mistakes."

BREAKING THE ICE

"When you're out walking and you see a funny looking car on the street, you can say to someone, 'That car looks like a giant M&M,

Meeting with Your Senior Managers

Here's a bold tactic that Julie Gilbert at WOLF Means Business has employed. "Early in my career, I had a boss who seemed sensitive about what meetings I should attend on my own or with him versus his attending on his own. It seemed strange because the project I was leading required me to be in on the discussion. So at one point, I asked him if he felt comfortable if I were to meet directly with some senior executives to garner more executive insight into the strategy we were working through. He couldn't say 'No' because my intentions were good and my outreach was only going to make the work better."

I asked Gilbert how my readers who work in large organizations could follow her lead. "I'd recommend that you go up a level or two, and you can call it an update, feedback, or get-to-know-you meeting. There's absolutely nothing wrong with doing it. It's being a good collaborator."

While Gilbert sounds fearless, she acknowledges that her approach has to be handled with finesse amid the politics of many organizations. "I broadened my network by having personal discussions with these senior leaders about big issues. And we got to know each other as human beings," she says. "I didn't make it all about work. I'd take 10 minutes to get to know who they are, whether they have kids, what their hobbies are, and how long they've been at the company. I gave them a reason to look me up or to connect with me in the hallway." Gilbert adds: "I could then ask about their kids, their running, or whatever it is."

doesn't it?' and the other person laughs, and you break the ice," says Jeanine Tesori, award-winning composer of the Broadway musicals *Caroline, or Change* and *Thoroughly Modern Millie*. "With these little innocent encounters—two or three sentences—you get to acknowledge that, 'Hey, we're on this planet together, and it's not so hard to talk to one another.' Practice breaking the ice in

Fan File

Make a file of everything complimentary people have said to you worth remembering. This "fan file" can include letters of recommendation, thank you notes, e-mails, and performance reviews from work. It can also include notes you jot down after particularly uplifting phone calls and meetings.

The idea is to aggregate the praise you receive and use it as a resource; you can also seek permission to quote some of the praise for testimonials on your Web site, in a brochure, or in other marketing materials. Your fan file can be helpful when crafting your elevator pitch as well as when writing cover letters, your résumé, and other materials that can help promote you. Refer to your fan file on a down day, when you don't believe you can do anything right. It's as if you open the file and it blows you a kiss!

everyday encounters, such as those with cab drivers and hairdressers. And don't be intimidated when talking to people with authority, like doctors and dentists."

Now for an all-purpose opening line that you can use at networking events. (An aside: Extroverts define all events as networking events—and that's something we can learn from.) It is the simplest, yet most effective, way to break the ice. Ready? Stand in front of a mirror, smile, and put out your hand, as if you were going to greet someone. Speak as if you own the room, and say: "Hello, my name is _____."

That's it. Nothing fancy. What you give off (e.g., confidence, intelligence, graciousness) is what people will pick up on. Nothing more and nothing less. Consider going to an event with someone more outgoing than you, who will help pave the path for you. If you can get someone to introduce you to others, it gives you immediate credibility. Learn in advance as much as possible about the event as well as who will be attending. Arrive early, so you can enjoy conversing before the room gets crowded and noisy. Doing so will also give you an opportunity to look at nametags and determine whom you'll want to speak with.

So you shake hands and bump heads (or fists!). Now what? Do you stare at your shoes? Pick lint from your pockets? Check your text messages? Not. How about taking the pressure and spotlight off yourself and focusing on the other person? Here are a few ways to get the conversation going:

- Prepare conversation topics before going to an event. One of my clients looks on Yahoo! and her other favorite news sources for the most frequently forwarded articles of the day.
- Make a positive comment about the speaker you just heard or about another aspect of the event.
- Ask open-ended questions, and avoid those that can be answered with a simple "yes" or "no," which can lead to thudding silence. Actively listen to the answers.
- Compliment something that your conversation partner is wearing that you like (faking it doesn't work).
- Ask for advice. People often enjoy talking about things they know about. For example, if your conversation partner is an actor, ask her about her favorite role that she's played and why it was her favorite.

The idea is to build rapport and get to know the other person—at least initially. "People respond well when you show interest in them," says Gary Osland at mNovakDesign. "And, while you may be uncomfortable in a networking situation, remember that many others often are too." He adds: "However, you're all there to connect in some way. And if you don't make it happen, you're wasting your time."

So smile and keep it positive, friendly, and not too personal, and avoid the usual off-limits topics such as religion, politics, and sex. "Socializing was an acquired skill," says Katharine Myers, coguardian and trustee of the Myers-Briggs Type Indicator Trust.

"I learned how to handle cocktail parties, but I don't do it as an extrovert. If I don't know anyone, I go up to a person who is alone and ask him or her a question. I show interest, and people like talking about themselves."

Another tip: Sometimes, when I'm feeling less energetic, I try to attract people to me rather than doing all the approaching. Here's how:

- I wear something that has a good track record as a conversation piece—say, a pendant or pin that often gets positive attention. The equivalent for men might be a tie with an interesting pattern or a pair of unusual cuff links.
- I prepare a few questions before attending a presentation. I make a point of asking one of them during the Q&A session. People often approach me afterward to discuss my question. We can circumvent the chitchat because we immediately have something thought provoking to discuss.
- In some cases, I take on the role of the organizer, host, or even the meet-and-greeter for an event to ensure that people can come to me and I can do less reaching out to them.

FLEXING YOUR NETWORKING MUSCLE

Julie Gilbert of WOLF Means Business shares how she networks at the gym. While Gilbert describes herself as "very extroverted," see what you can learn from her approach to networking and how you can apply it to your life: "I deliberately joined one of the most high-end gyms in the Minneapolis area because I'm running on the treadmill next to a CEO or an SVP in another company. And, inadvertently, over lifting weights or trading treadmills, I'm going to start talking to them, getting to know them, and building a network of people in our community.

"It's really simple. You just look up and give the person a nice smile and say, 'How are you doing today?' The first day you do that, the response is, 'Fine,' and the person moves on. The second day you do it, the person says, 'Fine,' again and moves on. The third day, the person is going to start talking to you. Build up a level of familiarity and trust by seeing each other in the same spot every day, and pretty soon, if you create the environment to engage in a conversation, the person will join you. If you jump them right away and ask them some big questions about solving world peace, the person is probably going to think you're crazy."

"SO TELL ME ABOUT YOURSELF"

You meet someone new. "So tell me about yourself," you say. Would you rather hear: (1) a robotic "I'm a systems analyst" type of response; (2) a 10-minute ramble; or (3) a succinct response that entices you to learn more?

An *elevator pitch* is the third option. While the concept may be as old as the elevator itself, the idea is to get across your message in the time span of an elevator ride. You can always say more once you entice the other party into conversation, or you can exchange business cards if there's mutual interest and time is short. "You really only have that first minute to establish your persona and determine if you're going to make a connection," says Gary Osland.

The delightfully named Twitpitch, which is the brainchild of "social tools" maven Stowe Boyd, takes the traditional elevator pitch a step further. It fits into the format of the microblog Twitter, which limits all communications via Web, cell phone, and instant messaging to 140 characters—approximately 20 words. Boyd refers to the Twitpitch as an escalator pitch because it can be said in 10 seconds, or the time it takes to pass someone going the opposite way on an escalator.[2] He stipulated other rules of engagement on his blog (www.stoweboyd.com) for vendors interested in pitching him. He doesn't waste a second!

I recently was inspired by the idea of superquick communications that pack a punch by *SMITH* Magazine (www.smithmag.net), the home of the "six-word memoir" ("Small kid, big dreams, Nobel Prize," by Cody Ybema). While a Twitpitch, or what we'll call a

Smithpitch, are fun exercises, it's fine to say your message in a few tight sentences. "Understand what makes you even just a little bit unique and accentuate that," says David Vinjamuri, author of *Accidental Branding*.

Even the most pithy elevator pitch works only when it's appropriate to your audience. So create at least one boilerplate version as a starting point, and tweak it depending on whom you're talking to. For example, I don't mention that I'm a coach right away to someone who might not be familiar with the profession; instead, I say what I actually do.

One of the boilerplate versions of my elevator pitch is: "I'm a mirror who reflects your best self, a sounding board for your deep intelligence, and a navigator to help your quiet star twinkle." Once I get my conversation partner's attention, I might add that, as a coach, I help people of a quieter nature present and promote themselves with more confidence. I might just say the latter if I'm talking to a more linear thinker. If I'm at a party talking to a creative person, I might say: "I make invisible people visible without smoke and mirrors or sawing anyone in half." At that point, I hope that the other person responds or asks me a question. If not, I might add the bit about being a coach—or just refresh my drink. Sometimes I say that I'm an executive coach because it's a better-known catchall phrase for what I do and it distinguishes my profession from life coaching. If I'm talking to another coach, I can just come out with it and say I'm a business communication coach, which is likely to evoke glazed eyes in other company. I avoid using the word *introvert* unless I have a sense that the other party will know what I'm talking about. So it all depends on who's listening.

Here are some more examples of elevator pitches:

I lead intrepid men and women on expeditions into uncharted emotional terrain. We fearlessly scale the highest peaks and traverse the deepest chasms. Our mission: to leave you on the edge of your seat.

—Barbara Rubin, theater director

Historical Figures' Elevator Pitches

Imagine taking an elevator with some historical figures (or passing them on an escalator!). I asked funnyman Carl Kissin to write their elevator pitches to further illustrate how much you can get across in so few words. Guess which historical figures they belong to? The answers are at the bottom of this page.

1. "It's funny that I'm pitching you, 'cause if you were pitching me, I'd hit it out of the park—and be the first black man to do so."
2. "I am committed to not fighting for what's right, which is my way of fighting for what's right."
3. "I'm all about fairness. Some stand up for what they believe in. I sit down."

And this is Carl Kissin's:

"Writes funny, writes fast, and is right for your writing needs. If you want to meet Mr. Write—Carlkissin.com."

I help leaders with people problems and people with leader problems.

—Dan Weber, executive and career transition coach

I enter a time machine and go back to the day of the dinosaur to explore supermassive black holes swallowing their surroundings in nearby galaxies a hundred million light-years away.

—Nancy Levenson, Ph.D., astrophysicist and professor, University of Kentucky

1. Jackie Robinson 2. Mahatma Gandhi 3. Rosa Parks

CRAFTING YOUR ELEVATOR PITCH

Now it's your turn. Think about what makes you exceptional (or what your greatest supporters would say), jot down a draft of your elevator pitch, be creative, have fun with it, put it away, share it with a trusted colleague, and keep noodling it until the words really sing who you are.

In the space that follows, write brief answers to each of the following questions. Keep in mind that the more specific you are, the more interesting your pitch is likely to be.

- What do you do?

  _____

  _____

- What's different about your approach?

  _____

  _____

- What problems do you solve, and for whom?

  _____

  _____

- What else would your prospective employers, clients, and other people in your network like to know about you? If you don't know, do some research—which is one of your strong suits as an introvert.

  _____

  _____

Now combine your responses and edit them to ensure that they flow and sound compelling. Imagine whittling down a piece of clay until it takes a desired shape. Say your elevator pitch out loud. Make an audio recording, or just leave yourself a voice mail so you can hear it. Practice saying your pitch to several friends or colleagues. Naturally, you will adjust it depending on whom you're speaking to since the content of your message is only half the battle. The other half is targeting your audience, which we discussed in the previous chapter. Analyze your audience and zoom in on its WIIFM—or its What's In It For Me. Lastly, consider when it's appropriate to use humor and creativity to show more of your personality.

BUSINESS CARDS

Don't leave home without your business cards. The big question is how and when to exchange them. I'm not a fan of offering business cards randomly (Spare the trees!) except at business meetings with people you've never met and in certain cultures in which it's the norm (e.g., Japanese). At the end of a satisfying conversation or even a positive brief exchange, you might say: "I really enjoyed meeting you. I'm going to mingle a little more right now, but I'd like to keep in touch. Would you like to exchange business cards?"

Next, what do you do with the business cards you collect? I like to send (and receive) a brief pleased-to-meet-you e-mail to cement the connection and leave the door open for future contact. While this step is not necessary, it can often be helpful to your new contact and you to remind both of you of your reason to stay in touch.

THE SKINNY ON PRESENTING YOURSELF WHEN YOU NETWORK

I met Chita Rivera after one of her shows. Her presence was dazzling, largely because her eye contact, like that of Bill Clinton and Earvin "Magic" Johnson, was deep and steady and it made our connection feel intimate during the brief time that we spoke. Everything counts when you're networking—from the quality of your voice to your posture to your handshake to your choice of clothing. Here are a few quick tips and reminders:

- Make eye contact. Research has shown, unsurprisingly, that "a direct, face-to-face position, along with eye contact . . . is thought to be a fundamental principle for effective communication." It has also shown that people who avoid eye contact tend to be more shy, or socially anxious, and introverted.[3] If that's you, practice looking people squarely in the eye when you speak to them. If that's too awkward for you, for social or cultural reasons, it's fine to look at your conversation partner's forehead or eyebrows for similar effect.
- Project your voice, vary your tone, and be conscious of speaking in a natural pitch. Get voice and/or presentation skills training if you need to speak more powerfully.
- Always be aware of your posture; stand or sit up straight, yet not stiffly.
- Use a firm and not crushing (or limp!) handshake.
- Dress and groom yourself impeccably, as if you were about to make an appearance on *The Today Show*.
- Contain your nervous energy. Be mindful of what you do with your hands, and particularly avoid fidgeting.
- Ask for feedback about how you present yourself from someone you trust and whom you consider to be polished and professional.
- You've probably heard that it's a good idea to be yourself. What does that mean? Be grounded, clear, and audience focused. Think of a time when you presented your best self.

Of course, not everyone plays nice when they're out networking. "I know someone who goes to cocktail parties and keeps an eye out for the famous people," says Michele Wucker, executive director of the World Policy Institute. "Of course, you've got to know whom you need to connect with. But this guy will stop a conversation midsentence if he sees somebody more important than the person he was talking to."

I know you won't do that. A key to networking is respecting the people in your presence. "People may not remember what you tell them, but they'll certainly remember how you made them feel," says Vincent Suppa, head of The Middle Way One World Company®.

Now that you know how to—and how not to—open more doors with a smile, genuine interest, and persistence, Chapter 6 will take you to the next step to expand your reach. Public speaking is one of the most valuable tools available to an introvert who is looking to increase her or his visibility. We'll take this topic, which can seem daunting, and break it down into accessible steps, once again focusing on your natural gifts as an introvert. Oh, and don't miss some amazing advice from Warren Buffett!

REFLECTIONS AND ACTIONS

What You Learned

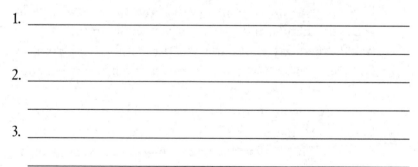

1. _____

_____

2. _____

_____

3. _____

_____

Action: What will you do?	How You'll Do It: What support or further information will you obtain?	Accountability: Whom will you tell about this action?	Completion Date: By when?

six

Your Chalk Talk

Public Speaking for Private People

For an introvert, giving a presentation off the cuff can be like starring in your own personal low-budget horror flick. A fierce wind blows. You're standing at the edge of a large black hole with a many-headed monster lashing its tentacles at you from the pit below. Your mind goes blank, your voice goes mum, and your presence fades into a shadow of itself as your mother tongue flies out the window. The monster rolls its eyes at your every utterance, the audio system roars at you, and purple flames lick at your feet.

Okay, maybe you don't imagine it quite that vividly, but public speaking can be scary. Just hearing the words "presentation" and "performance" provokes a primal fear in so many of us introverts. Do you naturally prefer quiet time in which to gather your thoughts, quiet people with whom to share them, or, best of all, solitude? Then how do you propel yourself from your comfort zone behind the scenes, put on a top hat, and run with the show?

I asked the Oracle of Omaha, Warren Buffett, for his thoughts (see Chapter 8 for details about how I came to speak with him and other luminaries). Buffett strongly relates to the introverts' experience and shares how he conquered his fear of public speaking: "I was absolutely terrified of public speaking in high school and college. I avoided courses where public speaking was required. I got physically ill even thinking about speaking."

"I signed up for a Dale Carnegie course," he says, referring to the performance-based training company known for its public speaking courses, "when I was a student at Columbia University. I gave them a check for $100—and went back to my room and stopped payment. You're looking at a real man of courage here." Some time later, when Buffett went back to Omaha, he signed up again. "This time I took $100 in cash. I joined a group of 30 people who had trouble saying their names."

After completing the course, Buffett volunteered to teach investment courses at the University of Omaha. "The ability to communicate both in writing and orally is enormously important. Most schools won't teach it because they consider it too simple. However, if you can communicate well, it's a big advantage." Isn't it comforting to learn that even Warren Buffett, who speaks eloquently off the cuff about everything from investing to the price of ethanol, has his own turnaround story as a public speaker?

While as introverts we're more at home in the private world of our thoughts and imaginations, many of us have surprising advantages in the outward world of public speaking. Our propensities for solo activities, such as research and deep thinking, for example, suit us well for stepping into the shoes of our audiences and carefully choosing our words. In this chapter you'll learn how to use your own specific advantages, whether you're giving an informal presentation to your peers or a speech at a conference.

First I'll share my advantages and challenges as a public speaker, and then we'll look at yours. You'll learn about three aspects of improving your public speaking, or presentation, skills (I'm using these terms interchangeably because they use the same skill sets): how to prepare, how to deliver your message, and what to do in a pinch. We'll once again reinforce your strengths rather than focus on what you're missing.

While you can read volumes about public speaking to learn the basic principles, I hope by the end of this chapter you'll start practicing what you've learned since there's no substitute for actually speaking. Most of what we'll cover will help you improve your public speaking skills, regardless of where you are on the introversion-extroversion continuum. I'll offer insights and tips of specific value to introverts. If you're already a seasoned public speaker, you'll probably still pick up a few useful techniques and reminders.

MY ADVANTAGES AS A PUBLIC SPEAKER

Here are the advantages I enjoy as a public speaker. See which ones you relate to.

1. **Preparing.** My key to public speaking with minimal anxiety is preparing. Some might call it overpreparing. That's fine. They can do it their way. Mine is to visualize my presentation, from the big picture to the font I choose for my visuals. I create a list of everything I need to do to get ready, which often includes checking out the room in advance, learning about members of my audience, and setting aside time to get grounded right before I'm "on." Like a locomotive, I'm fueled up and en route to my destination, and no matter what happens, nothing can derail me. Even if you're not naturally inclined to plan, I strongly recommend that you use some of your much-needed quiet time to prepare and rehearse for your presentations. Planning will not only help reduce your anxiety, but it also will enable you to tap into your introverted preference to think before you speak.

2. **Researching.** I enjoy rooting around the Internet and gathering facts, figures, and other gems to add sparkle to my presentations. As an introvert, I happily wander this unlimited terrain and feel at home in this solitary journey. When I'm ready, I can pick up the phone or venture out for additional input. Unlike my more extroverted cohorts, research energizes me. While they're out working the room, I'm in wandering around the wikis of the world.

3. Engaging in one-on-one conversations. "The art of presentation is the art of making a connection between you and every member of your audience—*all at the same time*!" says Vincent Suppa, Ph.D., head of The Middle Way One World Company®, a sustainable development organization. Likewise, I frame public speaking as a one-on-one conversation—with person A, person B, person C, and so on. As an introvert I like to be with individuals more than groups. So I frame my presentations in my head as if I'm talking to only you (and you and you and you), which is far easier than addressing the masses. I also prefer giving interactive presentations to speeches. Why? True to my introverted nature, I would rather get the audience talking so I can do less of it, and so all eyes aren't just on me!

4. Having the party come to me. As an introvert, I prefer to be approached rather than to approach. When I'm the speaker, I envision myself as the organizer or the connector. I'm the one whom everyone wants to know, the brain they want to pick, and the ear they want to bend. Not that I'd want that every minute of every day, but why not encourage an exchange of information while fostering connections among others and raising my visibility?

> When I was a young lawyer, the senior managers at the firm said to me: "If you want to become a trial lawyer, you'll have to develop a stage persona." Many actors, for example, are shy and inward in the real world, but they develop a persona that they're able to turn on when they're onstage. That allows them to project the confidence that the world sees and values.
>
> **—Ken Frazier, executive vice president and president of Global Human Health at Merck & Co., Inc.**

MY CHALLENGES AS A PUBLIC SPEAKER

1. **Preparing like crazy.**   You may be wondering why I included "preparing" as my first advantage, and "preparing like crazy" as my first challenge. The operative word is *crazy*. My natural inclination is to drive myself nuts before giving a presentation. In fact, each speaking gig can be a big ink blot on my calendar, and it's hard to relax in the time leading up to it. Hence, the challenge. My version of hell: Oprah's people invite me to appear on her show early the next morning. I stay up all night preparing—Googling and writing notes on my computer and on little square "stickies." I rehearse to myself at the airport, and practice and practice until I fall asleep. Then I recite my talking points out loud on the ride from O'Hare to her studio. I am ready, but I'm in a vaporous state of consciousness. While I told you earlier that preparing is one of my strong suits, I'll add that I struggle to balance it with getting a good night's sleep—a hazard of being an introvert and a perfectionist! "People ask me where I learned my public speaking," says the extroverted Cathie Black, president of Hearst Magazines. "I've been doing it forever and I practice." While she acknowledges that "an introvert is going to have a harder path," we also get the satisfaction of overcoming a big challenge when we speak to an engrossed audience.

2. **Being talked to when I'm off duty.**   If it were socially acceptable, I'd wear a sandwich board that says "Please don't talk to me" before I present, during breaks, and right afterward. These are the times when I like to be in my introverted bubble. As much as I try to be personable, I experience interactions as interruptions—of my thought process. The big "however" is that I don't want to alienate members of my audience and potentially lose valuable networking opportunities. So I negotiate the delicate balance between getting the quiet time I need and socializing. I like to arrive well rested so that the influx of people contact won't feel like a barrage.

3. **Not having the option to "undo."** As much as I find writing challenging, at least I can take my time and edit. Speaking is scarier in one way: Once I say something, I can't take it back. And it's far worse to misspeak in front of a roomful of people than over coffee with my best friend. I'd quickly lose my audiences if I labored over every word the way I do when I write. And I can only say "Let me think about that for a moment" so many times.

4. **Having nothing to say.** Nothing intelligible comes to the surface, and I can access only the flotsam drifting along my stream of consciousness. The brighter thoughts are down deep in the recesses. Maybe it's fear, maybe it's perfectionism, or maybe, as an introvert, I'm just not wired to spout out enlightening insights all the time. Arriving well prepared and consciously breathing help me the most.

Where to Sit at Business Meetings

It's as important to present yourself with aplomb when you're at a business meeting as when you're behind a podium. Cathie Black addresses the former: "Sit at the right place at the table. Introverts generally, and 98 percent of the time women, sit in what I call the four 'dead zones'—at the end of a table at each corner, as opposed to the end of the table facing into the table. That's the hardest place to hear anyone. Normally very strong people sit in the center and the bosses sit at the ends. So sit one place away from the center. Then, if you have something to say, it's not hard to do so from the center position, even if the first time you do so you'll feel like 'I don't belong here.' If you belong at the meeting, you belong in that seat."

YOUR ADVANTAGES AND CHALLENGES AS A PUBLIC SPEAKER

Now that we've talked about my advantages and challenges as a public speaker, it's time to entertain yours. Fill in the blank spaces in the following tables.

Your Advantages as a Public Speaker	How Can You Use These Advantages?
Example: You're a good writer.	*You can take your time to craft well-thought-out speaker's notes in advance to help you articulate your thoughts without the stress of thinking on your feet.*

Your Disadvantages as a Public Speaker	What You Can Do about Each of These Disadvantages
Example: You find it challenging to speak impromptu.	*You can take an improv class and join a local Toastmasters International group to get practice.*

PRESENTING TO BIGWIGS, HONCHOS, AND OTHERS WHO PUT ON THEIR PANTS ONE LEG AT A TIME

I have a client we'll call Manuel Vasquez who is an operations manager at a major nonprofit. As part of his job, he periodically gives presentations to his organization's board of directors. While he's normally a highly articulate and passionate presenter, Vasquez, who identifies as an introvert, gets intimidated in front of people he perceives as more powerful. By role-playing, exploring, and videotaping his mock presentations, we found what helps him: Vasquez is most confident when he thinks of himself as a professor. He loves to share his knowledge and thoughts. In fact, he plans to go back to school for a doctoral degree in organizational psychology and ultimately teach at a university. When he plugs into his professor persona and enters a meeting with the powers that be, he presents with more authority—verbally and nonverbally.

Another tactic to stay grounded when faced with More-Senior Powers That Be: View the interaction as a game. Use your deep thinking and research abilities as an introvert to figure out the rules and find the fun in overcoming this hurdle.

JITTERS

You may have heard that, for many people, the fear of public speaking trumps the fear of death. Since you die only once but you can give many presentations in your lifetime, why not make public speaking not only less frightful but actually enjoyable? While many introverts and extroverts alike struggle with giving presentations, we introverts have our own special struggles. Many of us loathe drawing attention to ourselves and speaking impromptu, and some of us are compelled to prepare to the point of exhaustion. We prefer the company of one person, or small groups to large groups, so the prospect of commanding an auditorium full of

people can be daunting. Finally, we may not be outwardly energetic by nature, and energy is what it takes to light up a room.

So where is all of this energy going to come from? While an
extrovert has a ready supply emanating from all the warm bodies
in the room, an introvert is fueled more by her inner world.
However, we can also get energy from a connection with one person in the audience. "If someone says something that sparks me
and then I spark him or her back, I often find that the whole room
comes along for the ride," says Anne Houle, a senior manager for
leadership training at Saks Fifth Avenue.

Before we delve into more tactics, let's take a moment to explore a
more inward pursuit that can pay huge dividends in your ability to
give a presentation calmly and in much better control.

MEDITATION AND SELF-PROMOTION—HUH?

Some people seem to be unflappable, as if they were born under the
shade of a palm tree on a warm, breezy day. I'm definitely not one
of them. As an introvert and a highly sensitive person living amid
the blinking lights, honking horns, and frantic pace of New York
City, I need to calm myself down every day to function at my best.
And what better way to find my own inner palm tree shade than
doing a little meditation? So why are we talking about meditation
in a book about self-promotion? Research at the University of
Kentucky shows that meditation is not only an effective way to
relax but it is also a way to enhance performance.[1]

A marathoner way back when, I've maintained a more moderate
lifelong exercise regimen in recent years; yet somehow, despite all
that fitness, something inside me was still a jumping bean. So I
discovered meditation, which quiets down and refreshes my mind.
And as an introvert, I'm particularly well suited for this solitary
practice, which primes me to do my best at public speaking—not

to mention networking, selling, negotiating, and even just managing the stresses of day-to-day life.

One of my clients, whom we'll call Harry Samuels, is a portfolio manager for a multi-billion-dollar investment portfolio, and he has been practicing meditation over the past 10 years. He teaches an investment class at a top-10 graduate business school. "Whether I'm presenting or having a conversation," he says, "when I am fully engaged, fully present and grounded, I'm totally open to what's unfolding at that moment." Samuels, who is an introvert, continues: "And so there's a real deep connection and a spontaneity that is nourishing internally. It's creative, and it's really at the heart of what's best about life. So if you are presenting, you're picking up naturally on all the subtleties of what's happening in the room, and the energy you're receiving or not receiving from other people." Samuels describes an additional benefit of meditating: "You're enjoying the experience much more than you would if you weren't fully grounded."

Samuels practices *mindfulness meditation*, which focuses on the breath to allow the mind to quiet down: "You start to see the thoughts arise and pass, and you don't cling to them as much. And as that process happens, your mind settles down, and you deepen into a more grounded place." He emphasizes: "It's been one of the most life-changing disciplines I've had."

Samuels asks his MBA students to try meditating; I do the same at the start of some of my presentation skills classes. I play a 10-minute guided meditation tape by Jon Kabat-Zinn, Ph.D., which helps relax many of my students through breathing and imagery before they present. Samuels says that his students who try meditating for the first time—even for 5 minutes—report a profound impact; they often say that time appears to slow down and that their thoughts become clearer. Coincidentally, Samuels recommends a book on guided meditation by Kabat-Zinn that I also adore: *Wherever You Go, There You Are.*

So meditation is a valuable tool that will help you enhance your overall well-being and equip you to manage so many of life's stresses, including public speaking. Vincent Suppa notes: "As an introvert, you're already inclined to go inward. So instead of fighting this tendency, use it to your advantage by performing one of the most ancient forms of preparation: Meditation!"

"One alternative to mindfulness meditation is to meditate with the *end in mind*," says Suppa, "which makes sense for many people in the business world. Visualize an already successful keynote speech prior to actually giving the speech." He adds: "The mind does not like dissidence, and if it imagines through meditation that you have already succeeded in your presentation, it will calibrate the parts of your external environment that are within your control for success."

In addition to heading his sustainable development organization, Suppa, who spent time training as a Buddhist monk in Southeast Asia, is a polyglot who speaks multiple European and Asian languages and is the director of human resources at a major international European conglomerate—all of which he had imagined that he had already succeeded at through meditation and visualization.

While you don't have to be a superachiever to meditate, the practice might just help you find the shade of your own inner palm tree and cause an uptick in your own performance.

HOW TO PREPARE

When I was a child, my father was an in-house doctor at the Metropolitan Opera House. In addition to the excitement of meeting the divas of the day, I was cast as an extra in *La Bohème*. The role required that I cross the stage on cue. The orchestra played in the pit below, the grand curtain rose, and grown-ups in elaborate costumes sang. But while the other young ragamuffins had already crossed the stage, I somehow missed the cue. Disoriented and horrified by my misstep, I scurried across the vast stage alone. Now, as a grown-up, it's clear that all I needed was to be better prepared.

How does this apply to you and your presentations? From creating failsafe speaker's notes to rehearsing aloud to checking out the venue in advance, you can arrive at a presentation ready to deliver your best. While there's no guaranteed formula for a flawless presentation, by learning the elements we're about to discuss, you'll find what's right for you. The more natural you are, the more you can relate to your audience, and the more relaxed everyone will be. Conversely, don't nervous people make you jumpy? Arrive at your presentation grounded so that you can be focused on your message yet relaxed enough to adjust on the spot. Once you hit your stride, you probably won't feel as if you're giving a big, scary presentation. Members of the audience, for their part, can get absorbed as if they're watching a captivating movie. The screen, the seats, and the exit lights fade into the background.

Even though I'm a plotter-planner and a perfectionist by nature, I sometimes find the preparation process daunting. Why? Gone unchecked, I would spend 100 hours planning for every hour onstage. However, that leads to a cranky, sleep deprived Nancy. So I've learned to compromise to keep my balance.

Building a Framework

Answer the following questions to build a framework to help you plan for many different types of presentations, including formal speeches at conferences and informal meetings at your place of work. Once you've mapped out these strategic essentials, the rest will fall into place more easily.

■ **Goal.**   What is the goal (or point) of your presentation? Do you want to inform, raise awareness, persuade, inspire, sell, encourage people to take action, build relationships, increase your visibility, or achieve something else?

■ **Key message.**   Write a one-sentence message you want your audience to walk away with from your presentation. Imagine an audience member briefly describing her or his takeaway to someone who didn't attend. What would she or he say?

■ **WIIFM.**   Tune back in to that imaginary radio station we talked about in Chapter 4. Remember to step into the shoes of your audience members and ask yourself from *their* perspective: "What's In It For Me?"

■ **Actions.**   What actions do you want your audience to take as a result of your presentation?

Evaluate Your Audience

Find out as much as possible about your audience in advance. "I recently did three commencement addresses," says Cathie Black. "I worked hours on each of them, thinking about the audiences and what I wanted to say. I talked to students in the graduating classes to get a feel for the schools. It may not look like it when you walk out there, but it takes preparation."

So who are the people in your audience? What do they have in common? What are their cultural backgrounds? What do you know about their demographics and preferences? What brings them to your presentation? Are they there by choice? Is it a small, intimate group of acquaintances or a stadium full of strangers? What is their mood likely to be—upbeat, friendly, suspicious, gloomy? Will they be tired after a long day's work or relaxed after a day at the beach? Are you presenting to them before bonus time or after a layoff announcement? The more you know about your audience, the better you can adjust your tone and fine-tune your message to make it relevant, appropriate, and timely. To delve deeper into evaluating your audience, refer back to Chapter 4.

Content

Assume that your audience has a short attention span. If you're not clear about your single key message, review all the points you want to make and distill them down into something memorable. It's fine if your first draft fills page after page; refine your thoughts until you're satisfied with your concise and compelling content.

It's pet peeve time. While I'm not completely anti-PowerPoint, I am against being numbed or overwhelmed by slide after slide of everything a speaker knows about a topic. On the other hand, I'm all for learning a few cool nuggets that the speaker supports with visuals (PowerPoint or otherwise) and then getting back to my business.

Edward Tufte, the professor who wrote the seminal booklet *The Cognitive Style of PowerPoint*, gives the Yale equivalent of a "Bronx cheer" to PowerPoint—definitely two thumbs down. In a *Wired. com* essay titled "PowerPoint Is Evil," Tufte says: "At a minimum, a presentation format should do no harm. Yet the PowerPoint style routinely disrupts, dominates, and trivializes content. Thus PowerPoint presentations too often resemble a school play—very loud, very slow, and very simple."

"The practical conclusions are clear," he continues. "PowerPoint is a competent slide manager and projector. But rather than supplementing a presentation, it has become a substitute for it. Such misuse ignores the most important rule of speaking: Respect your audience." Tufte favors giving handouts to audiences instead of presenting on PowerPoint, and he contends that bulleted points oversimplify our thoughts.[2]

"PowerPoint presentations are deadly," asserts Doug Fidoten, president of Dentsu America, Inc., a full-service advertising and marketing-communications company. "For introverts they can be even more deadly because the more words on the page, the more you're likely to default to reading what's up there and not making it come alive. The way to get around this: Use fewer words—so that there's almost nothing on the page." He adds: "Maybe the only thing is a visual image. That helps an introvert get into storytelling, rather than reading prepared text."

"Sometimes you have to do the PowerPoint stuff, but it's usually not such a good idea," says Craig Newmark, customer service rep and founder of craigslist. "Very importantly, brevity is the soul of wit." I attended an event at which Newmark gave a presentation without PowerPoint or other visual aids on how he started craigslist. The audience was rapt.

A client of mine whom we'll call Amy Jacobs offers a different perspective. In the investment bank where she's a technology vice president, it's the culture of the organization to share ideas using PowerPoint. "I find it easier to go to a meeting with a PowerPoint deck," she says, "because it gives everyone something to focus on. It doesn't have to be fancy—just some bullet points for me to speak to. They make my presentations more concrete."

Having spent more than a decade in the corporate world, I've seen my share of what Jacobs calls "decks," or PowerPoint presentations typically jammed with as many fonts, words, colors, and animated clip art as possible on each page. To make matters worse, when speakers used PowerPoint, the lights were often low, my eyelids would be heavy from the fast pace and long hours, and I would sometimes find myself having to fight the involuntary nod of my head. I know you won't subject your audiences to this. You'll be succinct, you'll offer them useful information and stimulate thought—and then you'll leave them wanting more.

It's natural to spend most of your preparation time creating your content rather than rehearsing your delivery. Without any direction, most of my clients and students would spend at least 90 percent of their time on content while neglecting to rehearse the nonverbal and vocal aspects of their presentations. That's a big "oops." Imagine if Martin Luther King, Jr., had delivered his historic *I Have a Dream* speech while hunched over a podium, mumbling in a monotone, and never looking up from his notes. What a striking contrast that would have been to his riveting delivery.

Preparing Your Presentation

What do you need to do more and less of—if anything—to create a memorable presentation? How much time do you have to prepare?

Let's say you have 12 hours over the course of two weeks. How much of that will you spend on research? On learning about your audience? On collecting input from others? On writing your speaker's notes? On creating charts? How about rehearsing? (Don't shortchange that one!)

When can you complete each aspect of the preparation? Would you do better by having everything ready a week in advance or by leaving most tasks until the last minute? What are your contingency plans if, say, your final rehearsal gets bumped because of a drop-everything priority at work?

Now think deeply about your message. Make it fresh and crisp. Remember to coordinate your message with your nonverbal communication. In fact, I often ask my clients to practice parts of their presentations without words to create, in effect, the silent movie before the talkie. Give it a try. You'll become more purposeful and conscious of how you gesture, move in the space, and coordinate with your visuals.

Speaker's Notes

Speaker's notes can be as invaluable to you during a presentation as GPS is when you're driving. They can help focus your presentation and remind you to say and do what you planned. Because they contain your key points and stage directions, speaker's notes keep you from getting nervous and losing your way so you get where you want to go. If you prefer to memorize your speech, be sure that your delivery sounds natural, and not canned. If you'd like to use notes, consider the following tips:

■ **Use index cards or letter-sized pages.**   If you're using index cards, I recommend a spiral-bound set rather than loose ones that you can drop or shuffle. If you prefer a letter-sized page format, staple or bind the pages together and type or write on only the top half of the page, which will prevent you from looking downward and losing eye contact with your audience.

■ **Use large text.** I typically use a 36-point font size, double spaced—with wide margins on both sides. Why do I like my notes so large? When I'm presenting, I'm not only focused on getting across my message but I'm also paying attention to cues from the audience. That doesn't leave a lot of room for finding my place on a page full of 10-point type. It's just like driving: it's vital to look up to stay connected to what's going on in front of you.

■ **Write yourself important reminders.** I include stage directions, such as "Go to pie chart," to remind myself when it's time to go to a different part of the stage and "Ask for scribe" when I want someone else—whom I've recruited in advance—to write on the flipchart or whiteboard. I also include on my speaker's notes reminders to breathe.

■ **Expect an onstage time warp.** Your presentation will probably take longer in front of an audience than it does when you rehearse. Imagine an astronaut walking in space. Your sense of time and the many things you need to keep track of may become compressed or otherwise distorted. Write time cues (e.g., 9 a.m., introduction and road map, or summary, of what you'll discuss; 9:15, first main argument; 9:30, second main argument; 9:45, recap and conclusion; 10, Q&A) on your speaker's notes to ensure that you cover all your points in time.

■ **It's fine to handwrite your notes.** I usually print out my speaker's notes and add handwritten notes in the margins.

■ **Only include the highlights.** In most cases, it's best to write summary points rather than every word you're going to say. Few people are adept at holding an audience's attention while reading a speech verbatim.

■ **Use color highlighters.** Doing so will remind you to emphasize your main points.

■ **Make a to-do list.** On the first page of your speaker's notes, include everything you must do upon arriving in the space where you'll be speaking. This list could include testing the equipment, setting up the room (e.g., moving the chairs into a semicircular formation for an interactive presentation), and placing handouts on the seats or in the front of the room.

■ **Write down everything you'll need to bring to the presentation.** Pack a bag with the following: Small hard candies without wrappers (e.g., Tic Tacs, Altoids) to help you in the event of a coughing attack, a handkerchief, backup garments (in case your originals get rumpled or stained at a meal), a bottle of water in case none is provided, extra markers, and tape. It may sound like overkill to lug so many items; however, you'll be thankful that you did on the occasion when you need them.

■ **Affix a brightly colored front and back cover onto your speaker's notes.** Doing so will ensure that your notes stand out among a sea of white paper and they don't get lost in the shuffle.

■ **Surround yourself with backups!** E-mail copies of your speaker's notes—and your presentation slides—to yourself as well as to the event organizer. Also carry copies on a flash key (i.e., a jump drive). Print out an extra hard copy of everything, and keep it separate from your original.

■ **Use your laptop as a teleprompter.** Doug Fidoten suggests an alternative to using speaker's notes on paper: "Say you're doing a presentation and it's being projected on the screen behind you. Set up your laptop in front of you. You do not need to look at the screen. You have, if you will, your teleprompter right there. It's a safety net if you lose your way or if something goes horribly wrong."

Rehearse

Unless you've studied acting, you may not fully appreciate the value of running through your presentation out loud in advance, again and again, until it's impeccable. By knowing your material cold, you'll free yourself up to handle all the unexpected variables that could arise. Here are some tips:

▪ **Have a technical rehearsal with all of the audiovisual aspects in the venue where you'll present.**   You may be surprised at how different it feels to deliver your presentation from behind a lectern in a brightly lit boardroom versus at the coffee table in your living room. If it's not possible to rehearse in the venue, at least visit it prior to your presentation to check out the room layout, the seating possibilities, the acoustics, the technical capabilities, and so on.

▪ **Rehearse out loud.**   Practice delivering your message along with your hand gestures, movements, and visual aids.

▪ **Practice in front of a mirror.**   Though it may seem contrived, standing in front of a full-length mirror and paying close attention to your facial expressions, gestures, and other movements will help you pinpoint what you need to work on in real time.

▪ **Videotape yourself.**   Take note of how you look when you're "on," and focus on ways to improve the physical aspects of your presentation. While practicing in front of the mirror and videotaping yourself may sound frightful because doing so may increase your self-consciousness, many of my clients and students consider both tools invaluable. Once you get past the initial discomfort, it can actually be motivating to see concrete evidence of your progress.

■ **Ask a trusted colleague, mentor, or coach to watch you.**
Invite her or him to critically assess your rehearsal, first by reinforcing what you did right and then by adding constructive comments. Specify the criteria you want to focus on (e.g., eye contact,
hand gestures, tone of voice, avoiding verbal filler such as "um,"
"er," "you know," and "like I said") to help focus the critique.

■ **Practice speaking extemporaneously.** Doug Fidoten
offers a novel approach to rehearsing from his early days as a presenter: "Behind the scenes when I practiced, I'd stand in a room and
speak. I went as long as I could until I faltered or just didn't know
what to say next. I started over again. I did it time and time again
until I could get from one end to the other and feel comfortable that
I knew what I wanted to say. That gave me confidence, even if I
might have sound bites or bullet points I was referring to. I no longer
find this necessary. Now I prepare what my talk is going to be with
bullet points and visual illustrations, and I simply talk to that."

■ **Wear a lavaliere-friendly outfit.** If you're going to use a
lavaliere mike, it might be best to wear clothing with a waistband,
such as a pair of pants or a skirt. The clips that hold the electronic
gizmo connected to some lavalieres don't hold on many dresses, or
even lapels. They clip on more securely to heavier fabrics.

■ **Have a dress rehearsal.** Change into everything you'll
wear at your presentation, from head to toe. When I've skipped
this step, I've had some unpleasant surprises: I never realized that
my new shoes clack loudly on a bare floor or my finest suit limits
the mobility of my hand gestures.

■ **Manage the space.** When you rehearse in the venue, determine where you'll stand and move. Will you use a podium, lectern,
or half-lectern for your speaker's notes? Will you have an easel for
your flipchart? Is there a whiteboard? Will you need a mike, and if
so, will it be a tiny clip-on lavaliere mike, which will free up both

of your hands, a handheld mike, or a podium mike? Will you have a choice?

▪ **Test the audiovisual equipment in advance.** Test it again when you enter the room. I arrive at least an hour early to do a sound check and make sure I know how to use the equipment. I arrange this in advance with the event organizer.

▪ **Determine who will be the point person during your presentation.** This person will be in charge of handling all the unpleasant things that can go wrong, including glitches with the audiovisual equipment and spikes in the room temperature.

▪ **Know when enough is enough.** A few of my clients claim that rehearsing too often actually detracts from their performance. Get to know what level of rehearsal enables you to present at your strongest.

Get Grounded Right Before You're On

Now that your presentation is prepared and you've checked out the venue, how can you get grounded before stepping onstage? Many of us have different approaches to reinvigorating our confidence and feeling refreshed and alert. For some, it's a physical activity, like taking a long walk. For others, it's relaxing our minds by doing yoga, meditating, or listening to relaxing music. "A good speech becomes a great speech when it really sounds like you," says Cathie Black. That happens when you're relaxed enough to connect to your core.

You may also want to try the following:

▪ **Write your first few lines on your speaker's notes.** "Speaking in public paralyzed me," says Katharine Myers, coguardian and trustee of the Myers-Briggs Type Indicator Trust. "When I was president of APT (Association for Psychological Type), I always had my first few sentences written down, since I was in fear of being speechless." A good alternative: Some of my clients swear by memorizing the first few lines of their presentations. Myers adds: "Because I had to, I gradually learned to relax and be myself, knowing I would never be a great speaker, but my belief in what I was saying would make it okay. If I lived again, I would take voice and public speaking training."

■ **Imagine a time you felt your strongest.**   Hold onto that feeling and visualize the most positive outcome of your presentation.

■ **Think about your unique strengths.**   It might help to review your affirmations before you go on.

■ **Take a few deep breaths before you begin to speak.**   We often forget, especially when we're nervous, to simply breathe. While I'm sure you're technically breathing, if your breath is shallow and scared, guess how your voice will sound?

Take Your Time

Watch how many speakers get onstage and start a speech before they get to the podium. Instead, take your time, walk across the stage, put your notes on top of the podium, plant your feet, and breathe. That may seem like an endless amount of time, but it works to your advantage. People sit up and pay attention before you even start talking. If you're talking as you walk across the stage, you're not looking at the audience, so you're not directing your message. It's okay to take your time to collect yourself.

—**Cathie Black, president of Hearst Magazines**

HOW TO DELIVER YOUR MESSAGE

You say so much before you even utter a word. The way you look at your audience, gesture, stand, move, and use your voice conveys volumes. The following is a snapshot of some of the most important things to remember about how you express yourself nonverbally before, during, and even after you deliver your message. Of course, looking someone directly in the eye is not acceptable in some cultures, and speaking succinctly is frowned upon in others. Adapt what's useful and appropriate to you and your audiences.

Eye Contact

It's amazing how so much connection can happen through such a small part of the body. Look at one audience member at a time for several seconds, and square up your shoulders with hers or his when you do. This doesn't initially feel natural to most people I've coached. However, it makes a significant difference in your ability to connect with your audience. It takes practice.

If you're rehearsing in a room alone, you can designate chairs to represent people that you'll look at for a phrase at a time. You can also practice this skill in your day-to-day life—at meetings or even when you're out to dinner with friends. If you're too uncomfortable making eye contact, look at people's foreheads or eyebrows for a similar effect. If you can't see your audience because of the lighting, it's still effective to look into the audience as if you're connecting with one pair of eyes at a time. The next time you attend a presentation, notice whether the speaker is making eye contact or is just scanning the room. How does the speaker's use of eye contact impact you?

Hand Gestures

If you use your hands when you speak in daily conversation, use your hands when you present. You will look natural and expressive. Make open gestures, keeping your hands away from your body, above your waist level, and out, as if you were embracing your audience. Avoid fidgeting, touching your clothing, putting your hands in your pockets, or leaning your arms on a podium, lectern, or other object.

Another word about podiums: If you have a choice, consider speaking without one—or at least using the podium as a starting point and then moving closer to the audience if the space permits it. While you may find comfort in having a stable place for your notes, most podiums block much of your body and even part of your hand gestures from the audience's view, which can make your presentation appear more static.

Make gestures to emphasize your points; however, avoid appearing like an orchestra conductor. If you're holding an electronic clicker to advance your slides, hold it steady in one hand. Place your hands to your side as a neutral position.

Watch videos of speakers you admire, determine what looks best about their hand gestures, and then find your natural best way of supporting and punctuating your words with your hands by practicing in front of a mirror. Of course, take into account the differences between gesturing to a live audience and gesturing to a camera in a tight frame for a TV interview.

Posture and Stance

While you don't have to be America's next top model, it would be helpful to rehearse your presentation with a book on your head because it will reinforce how it feels to stand and walk with your head up and spine well aligned. Elongate your spine by thinking of your head as a helium balloon floating up toward the ceiling. Relax your shoulders—when we're nervous they tend to creep up toward our ears. Keep your knees soft so they don't lock up. Relax your jaw. Plant your feet the width of two fists apart, and ground them squarely on the floor. If you tend to sway or shift from foot to foot, place one foot slightly in front of the other to help anchor you. Look at yourself in a full-length mirror. What do you need to adjust? If you're holding your breath, relax and take a big breath in, and then let it out along with your worries.

Moving with Purpose

I find it distracting when speakers pace around the stage or shift their weight from foot to foot. It's much more effective when speakers move in sync with their words—and walk only when they have a reason to do so. Avoid looking wooden by standing still in one place for your entire presentation. If you're not comfortable with moving onstage, take a few dance classes to build your confidence in your ability to move and express yourself nonverbally.

Voice

Here's another topic that you can spend a lifetime studying. "Introverts have a tendency to speak more slowly and quietly. As a result, we can feel that we've said something and no one has heard it or acknowledged it. It can make us feel invisible," says Katharine Myers. Unless your voice is already an asset, improve it by taking classes or private lessons; if you have a more serious challenge, like a stutter or a lisp, then consult with a speech pathologist.

"Learn to speak in a relatively strong voice, or your ideas are going to be passed over, and that's frustrating," says Cathie Black. She recommends practicing by speaking into a tape recorder. "It sounds very different. You might think to yourself, 'Oh, I didn't know that I sounded like a mouse!'" Think of someone whose voice you admire. What aspects of her or his voice are most appealing to you? What about your voice would you like to improve? A few reminders:

- Speak up.
- Vary your tone, rhythm, and even occasionally your volume.
- Speak at your natural pitch—when you're nervous, your pitch tends to go up.

- Enunciate.
- "Punch" important words for emphasis.
- Ensure that your body language, including your facial expressions, is in sync with your voice.
- If you misspeak and it's minor, keep going; if it's major, calmly and gently correct yourself. By breathing and strengthening your voice, you will become a much more powerful speaker.

WHAT TO DO IN A PINCH (THINK ST. BERNARD WITH A KEG OF PUBLIC SPEAKING CURE-ALLS)

You're ready. You've filled your flipchart with arresting visuals and powerful statements in advance. Your PowerPoint slides are concise and dynamic. It's show time! In this section we'll address two distinctly different sets of pitfalls. The first is within you—your hands shake, your mouth goes dry, and your feet become possessed, as if they're doing the Texas two-step. The second is external—the mike goes blooey, the computer acts viral, and the candy wrapper crackles while participants in the front row are checking their BlackBerrys. The following tips will help you focus on your presentation rather than on your jitters.

Managing Your Internal World

■ **What is your emotional state?**   Are you enjoying the experience or dreading it? Your audience can detect dread in your body language and hear it in your voice. Find ways to enjoy the experience. Remember your purpose for giving your presentation: it's probably something like sharing information, helping people, and building your business—and nothing diabolical! Remember again: Breathe.

■ **Touch your middle finger to your thumb.**   Doing so will help ground those shaky hands.

■ **Take your time.**   Don't rush to speak. You'll appear more confident if you pace yourself, rather than spitting out your whole speech in one breath.

■ **Avoid fidgeting.**   Only move to enhance your delivery.

■ **Make eye contact with a few friendly faces.**   Sustain this eye contact with each individual for several seconds while you square up your shoulders with hers or his. Focus on these physical aspects of your presentation, rather than on what people are thinking of you.

■ **Take sips of water.**   Drinking water will keep your throat hydrated and enable you to pause at points during your presentation.

■ **Avoid wasting energy trying to please your audience.** Find satisfaction in what you're doing inside yourself. Emotions are contagious. Echoing the first point, if you emanate genuine joy, enthusiasm, or passion, your audience will catch it.

Managing Your External World

If something goes awry, remember that your reaction sets the tone. Be calm, confident, and good humored. If you appear nervous, your audience is more likely to treat you like a substitute teacher minding a third-grade class. Here are a few tips to help you manage the unexpected.

■ **Stop the long-winded question asker.**   If an audience member starts giving a speech during the Q&A, politely interrupt and say, "In the interest of time, I'd like to go straight to your question." State your ground rules up front. For example: "We have time for a few questions in the next 15 minutes. Please make your questions succinct. If you'd like to chat with me more, I'll be available afterward, during the reception."

▪ **Stay cool amid difficult questions.** A corollary to the above point: If an audience member zings you with a difficult question, handle it coolly, and remember that nobody knows everything. If you're not sure how to answer, say so and offer to get back to the question asker at a later time. If you need a moment to think of your answer, you can briefly comment on the question. The line "That's a great question" is overused, but it works fine to buy you a moment to collect your thoughts in a pinch.

▪ **Know when to ask for help.** If anything goes wrong on the audiovisual front, stay calm, and if you can't immediately address the problem, ask for help. It's best to have someone lined up in advance to help you in these situations.

▪ **Keep moving forward, even if you miss something.** If you miss one of the points on your speaker's notes, unless it's a critical idea, ignore it and move on. If it's vital to your presentation, continue with your train of thought, then go back and mention the point later.

FAQS

Now that we've discussed so many different aspects of giving a presentation, I'll share my answers to the questions I'm most often asked.

1. **Question.** How would you like to be introduced?

    Suggestions. If you introduce yourself, say a few lines that are relevant to your audience. Distribute your bio in advance when appropriate. If someone else is introducing you, specify how you'd like to be introduced. Avoid asking the introducer to read your bio (zzzz . . .). Instead, you could share a few brief items, such as your title and one piece of information that would interest your audience. Make sure the introducer knows how to pronounce your name.

2. **Question.** What's an effective way to begin my presentation?

Suggestions. Get the audience's attention immediately. Don't fall into the trap of starting with a lot of thank yous. Yawn. Think Academy Awards acceptance speeches. Start with a surprising statistic, a piece of news, a quotation, or an anecdote to engage your audience. Jokes are risky, and sometimes they work. You can also start with a question, as long as it draws in your audience.

3. **Question.** How can I structure my presentation?

Suggestions. I like this simple, time-tested formula: Say what you're going to say (or your road map), deliver the heart of your message, and finally, summarize what you've said. I also like when a speaker uses numbers to give me a sense of where we're going. For example: "I have three points about the state of the economy: First, ... Second, ... And finally, third, ..." Along the way I enjoy hearing stories, statistics, and facts that support the main message. I usually have more attention for interactive presentations than speeches. However, speeches have their place. Structure your presentation to bring out the best in your style, message, and the expectations of the audience.

4. **Question.** How can I use visual aids to enrich my presentation?

Suggestions. Charts, graphs, tables, and pictures can add variety to your presentation and can help you make your point. While saying that revenues are up by 15 percent can be effective, supporting that statistic with a chart containing a diagonal line pointing upward will have even more impact, especially among people who are more visual. If you're speaking to a small group— say, fewer than 30 people—it's often effective to use a flipchart, whiteboard, or blackboard to underscore your points with notes as you're speaking. In these instances, prior to the presentation recruit a "scribe" to write notes up front, quickly and clearly, while you're presenting. This way you won't turn your back to the audience. If you're speaking to a larger group, PowerPoint can be fine (if you must!), as long as you follow the guidelines I'm about to address.

5. **Question.**   How many PowerPoint slides should I create for a 30-minute presentation?

Suggestions.   While the answer depends on so many variables, I generally recommend limiting your presentation to no more than 10 clean, simple slides, with a maximum of four bullets per slide. If you'd like to share more supporting materials with your audience, you can include them in handouts, e-mail them before or afterward, or post them on a Web site. One of the biggest mistakes I've seen in PowerPoint presentations is slides crammed with information that's too hard for the audience to comprehend or even see. *A quick note on positioning yourself when presenting with PowerPoint:* remember to always face your audience rather than turn toward the projection screen to point to the slides as you present them.

6. **Question.**   How interactive should my presentation be?

Suggestions.   Start by asking yourself which mode of delivery would bring out the best in your speaking abilities—a lecture, an interactive discussion with the audience, a panel discussion with other speakers, or even a fireside-chat style of discussion with an interviewer. While you won't always have an option, it pays to think about which approach would provide the most value to the audience. Ask for guidance in advance from the organizer whenever possible. Inquire about what's worked best in the past and what the audience prefers. However you decide to proceed, share a road map for your presentation with your audience toward the beginning. After your opening lines, tell your audience how much time you have and what you've planned for that time. You can also ask for input from the audience to ensure that your plan is in sync with their interests, when appropriate. If you'd like to entertain questions throughout your presentation, then say so. The downside of doing so is that the questions can interrupt the flow of your presentation and derail your agenda. The upside, however, is that having a dialogue with the audience helps ensure that you're on the same page throughout your presentation. You can also ask your audience to hold all questions until a Q&A at the end.

7. **Question.** What's an effective way to end my presentation?

Suggestions. End with power, presence, and purpose. Wrap up with a finale. Summarize what you've said. If your presentation is interactive, ask the members of your audience for their key takeaways. You'll learn what your audience actually absorbed, which may not be what you expected.

We've covered a lot in this chapter, from looking at our advantages and challenges as public speakers to the internal and external aspects of getting ready. While preparing thoughtfully will help, the best way to improve your skills as a public speaker is to get out there and do it. Not that you have to schedule a gig at Madison Square Garden.

Book a speaking engagement. Start with a small audience, possibly as part of your volunteer work. Some of my clients prefer to have a close friend in the audience as a smiling face they can count on to help anchor them. Others prefer presenting to strangers. Find the easiest way for you to get started. Determine what kind of presentation you'll develop, and create a plan. If you need to get more practice before your first speaking gig, join your local Toastmasters International group, take public speaking classes, or hire a presentation skills coach. Watch videos of outstanding speakers—you'll find plenty on the Web on *Ted Talks*, the Washington Speakers Bureau, and YouTube, including the speeches at the U.S. Democratic and Republican National Conventions. Have your presentations videotaped so you can continually improve. Solicit feedback (e.g., through evaluation forms) from audience members. Whatever you do, never lose sight of the strengths—introverted and just plain human—that make you a good speaker. It's fun to do something you're good at, and it can be even more rewarding to tackle something that's always been a challenge.

Using what you learned about presentation skills as a foundation, in the next chapter you'll learn how you can ace job interviews as an introvert. Regardless of whether you're currently looking for a job, you'll find tips, techniques, and reminders that you can apply to meetings and other typical business encounters.

REFLECTIONS AND ACTIONS

What You Learned

1. _____

_____

_____

2. _____

_____

_____

3. _____

_____

_____

Action: What will you do?	How You'll Do It: What support or further information will you obtain?	Accountability: Whom will you tell about this action?	Completion Date: By when?

seven

Your Job Search

Interviewing for Introverts

The recruiter, the hiring manager, and human resources have vetted you on paper. You've mustered enough verbal and vocal oomph to get past the Powers That Be by phone. Now it's time for you to meet in person. So how do you want to show up?

Of course, you want to be yourself, but you don't want to stare into space, pondering each question—while the interviewer thinks about lunch. In this delicate dance of protocol, etiquette, and introversion, one thing is clear: How well you connect with the interviewer in the next hour can determine whether you'll be spending more time with each other than with your loved ones in the years to come.

This speed-dating-like approach to managing your career can be daunting, particularly for an introvert. Why? It's harder for you to display the inner workings of your mind in real time than it is to craft a finely edited e-mail at your own pace. You would rather get to know the interviewer gradually than subject yourself to her or his invasive questions on the spot. However, when you're interviewing, you have to respond quickly, and every word counts—and can have a profound impact on your future.

Whether you've been sitting in the same cubicle for the past decade, are seeking a job with a bigger corner office, or feel stagnant at your current job and are mulling over your career advancement options, now is a good time to freshen up your interview skills. These skills are also important if you freelance or run your own company.

Of course, interviews are just one aspect of your job search. My introverted clients and students typically have no problem researching organizations and industries and mapping out strategies for their job searches. The part they need the most assistance with is fine-tuning their interview skills—so that will be our focus in this chapter. We already talked in Chapter 3 about your marketing mix, or the combination of activities you chose to help you raise your visibility. Even if you're not currently searching for a job, it pays to stay in touch with colleagues and line up informational interviews throughout your career to enhance your network and your knowledge of various organizations, industries, and trends.

In this chapter I'll describe the elements of a successful interview, with advice from senior managers and recruiters from a variety of fields. We'll discuss the importance of being authentic and enthusiastic as well as the power of listening carefully and describing what contributions you can make. Then we'll cover how to prepare for interviews, including how to analyze your audience and polish your résumé; we'll also review what to bring and wear. We'll talk about fine-tuning your nonverbal communication, preparing for the toughest questions, following up, and, when the time comes, negotiating your compensation.

While interviewing is a broad topic with volumes written about it, in this chapter we'll focus mainly on those aspects that are most relevant to introverts. I'll distill what I've learned from my experiences as both an interviewee and interviewer at different turns in my career. I'll also offer insights from my current work as a business communication coach who prepares introverted clients from diverse backgrounds for interviews at a wide range of corporate, nonprofit, academic, and governmental organizations.

INTROVERTS' CAREER CHOICES

Is your career choice well suited to your personality? Do you have to be "on" constantly, or do you get sufficient quiet time to process your thoughts on the job? "You'll find introverts in all walks of life," says Shoya Zichy, author (with Ann Bidou) of *Career Match*. "However, you'll find that more of them seek professions such as biologists, engineers, computer programmers, economists, and writers. These occupations require that people spend more time alone rather than working in teams." In contrast, she says that typically extroverted career choices include emergency room technicians, nonprofit directors, real estate managers, sportscasters, and politicians. You can probably see why introverts might steer clear of these more hectic and boisterous positions. What would you be most comfortable doing for a living?

Many of the 30 fastest growing occupations—according to projections by the Bureau of Labor Statistics for the period from 2006 to 2016—seem like a natural fit for us introverts, given our preference to dive deeply and quietly into the world of ideas and concepts. These occupations include network systems and data communications analysts, computer software engineers, personal financial advisors, veterinarians, and pharmacy technicians.[1]

My own personality is ideally suited to being a business communication coach. Now, in my life after Wall Street, I do the things I love for a living: listening, building deep one-on-one relationships over time, strategizing, and problem solving with my clients. All of these activities play to my introverted strengths. None of them tax me; in fact, they energize me.

I hope that you're doing what you love for a living. If not, I encourage you to take steps in that direction—or at least find a way to include activities that you enjoy during your personal time. If your current job is just paying the bills or getting you through an economic downturn, I would like to hold out a ray of optimism: if you adeptly and persistently aim at a career that's well suited to your personality and strengths, you'll get there.

The classic *What Color Is Your Parachute?* by Richard Nelson Bolles can help you explore your career options and strengthen your search. A book that speaks to those of us who have more than one profession, or "slashes," is *One Person/Multiple Careers* by Marci Alboher. If you're on a corporate track and daydreaming about your next steps, take a look at *Escape from Corporate America* by Pamela Skillings. You might check out a couple of career books specifically for introverts: *Careers for Introverts & Other Solitary Types* by Blythe Camenson and *200 Best Jobs for Introverts* by the editors at JIST and Laurence Shatkin, Ph.D. Also take a look at the work of Sharon Good, including her e-book *The Tortoise Workbook*, whose gentle and sage approach of helping you get ahead at your own pace is a natural fit for many introverts. Of course, some of these authors also have useful information on their Web sites and blogs as well. You may also consider hiring a career coach or counselor to help you think through your strategy.

Once you've had a chance to map out where you want to go with your career—or at least with your next steps—we'll explore how you'll get there. Just as there's not one right way to present yourself, there's not one right way to interview, nor is there just one type of interviewer. As long as you're prepared, articulate, and audience focused, you're at least likely to be taken seriously as a candidate. Since the goal of this chapter is to help you interview and get the job, I'll share plenty of tips and insights, and I encourage you to practice and hone your skills as we go.

SEARCHING FOR A JOB: YOUR ADVANTAGES AS AN INTROVERT

Searching for a job can be cumbersome—especially for introverts who lose their jobs in an economic downturn or amid the bloody battles of office politics. In fact, employees in management, business, and financial operations occupations who lost their jobs between 2005 and 2007 took an average (median) of six weeks to find a new job, according to the Bureau of Labor Statistics.[2] While those were relatively strong years with low levels of unemployment, during the economic slowdown in the period between 2001 and 2003, it took nine weeks. While you might think that introverts would have a harder time finding suitable jobs, it's safe to say that introverts and extroverts alike who spend time developing their networks over time find jobs more quickly.

Even if you shudder at the thought of having to "extrovert" your way through round after round of interviews, I'd like to offer you hope and encouragement. While it can be time-consuming, emotionally taxing, and even expensive (e.g., buying new interview suits), the interview process can lead you to a position that is better matched to your temperament, skill set, lifestyle, and financial needs. So whether you see interviewing as a dreaded means to a desirable end or you just gain satisfaction from taking on a challenge, being an introvert does not have to be a handicap in your job search—in fact, in many ways it's an asset. You can use your strength at researching to learn about the hiring organization and your interviewers. By using your ability to think deeply, you can write out and practice articulating how you can use your expertise to benefit the organization. By doing so, you stand a good chance at setting yourself apart from the other candidates and getting the offer.

Let's start by identifying the essentials of an interview that goes well.

ELEMENTS OF A SUCCESSFUL INTERVIEW

Your professional expertise is a given for your résumé even to land in the interviewer's "maybe" pile. If you're a private eye, you know your sleuthing, and if you're an ornithologist, you know your birds. If you don't know your stuff cold, determine what's missing, how and when you'll fill in the gaps, and even what you can do to gain an advantage over the other candidates.

Position yourself as an expert in your field—the brain, the whiz, the one who reads everything, is up on the buzz, the one with the answers. Having a strong command of your area of expertise is not negotiable. Get it, grow it, and share it. You don't have to flaunt it to be effective on interviews. However, being—or at least acting!—confident in your expertise will give you an edge. Another piece of advice: "Don't be self-deprecating when sharing information and expertise," says actuary Michael Braunstein, ASA, MAAA, who is responsible for actuarial talent management at Aetna Inc.

Now let's look at some of the more critical elements of successful interviewing. Remember: Be authentic, be enthusiastic, listen carefully and ask good questions, and describe what contributions you can make. Here's more about each.

Be Authentic

I bet you can tell the difference between someone who is being authentic and someone who puts on airs. So can your interviewers. Of course, it can be a delicate balance between showing your true self—with all the richness that implies—and acting appropriately. What does it feel like to be authentic? Putting your feet on the desk and playing air guitar? While that may be an expression of the real you, let's dig a little deeper. Think about what you're like when you're true to your values and you're not wasting energy trying to impress anyone.

As an introvert, you may enjoy going inward to ponder the following.

Describe when you're being your most authentic. Are you relaxing with your family on a weekend? Having a deep conversation with a close friend? Promoting a cause you're passionate about? Something else?

_____

_____

Describe when you're being your least authentic. Is it when you're trying to impress a room full of senior managers? Working the room at an office holiday party? Introducing someone you don't respect to an audience of peers? Something else?

_____

_____

Write the names of three people you know or fictional characters whom you think of as typically authentic or inauthentic in the space that follows. When I ask my clients to give me an example of someone who comes across as authentic, 9 times out of 10 they say Oprah Winfrey. She appears sincere, connected to her guests, and true to her emotions. She never seems phony. An example of a character that comes across as inauthentic is Troy McClure, the self-important has-been actor on *The Simpsons*.

Authentic People	What Makes This Person Seem Authentic?
1.	
2.	
3.	

Inauthentic People	What Makes This Person Seem Inauthentic?
1.	
2.	
3.	

Now that you've thought about why the people or characters you chose come across as authentic or inauthentic, let's bring this exercise back to you. Answer the following:

What makes you authentic or inauthentic?

_____

_____

What could you do to be more authentic, especially in a high-stakes situation such as a job interview?

_____

_____

Be Enthusiastic

This may date back to junior high: At a certain age, it became important to be cool. We can easily forget that it's okay to show enthusiasm, especially in a situation as stressful as a job interview. You may be concerned about coming across as too eager or, worse, desperate. Then you might overcompensate by seeming neutral or disinterested in the position or the organization. Furthermore, as an introvert with a well-developed and private inner world, you may be circumspect about showing emotion, especially to people you don't know well.

Keep in mind that emotions—including enthusiasm— are contagious. If the hiring manager's decision is between an effervescent you and an equally qualified bored or indifferent candidate, who do you think will get the offer? What's really important? "I can answer that with a single word: Passion," says Janet Riesel, SPHR, an associate director and senior recruiter at Ernst & Young. "I must see that the candidate really wants this specific job—not just a job at Ernst & Young. The prepared and motivated candidate won't only ask standard questions but will also show that he or she has researched the position and is really interested."

Let's say you're not entirely enthusiastic about a job but would like to get an offer to provide you with options so you can think about the opportunity further. Rather than seeming as if you're on the fence during the interview, focus on an aspect of the job about which you're genuinely excited. This positive emotion could spark possibilities that would not have been ignited had you come across as dispassionate. And possibilities lead to other possibilities.

Listen Carefully and Ask Good Questions

We all want to be heard, but a surprising number of people only half-listen. This holds true in an interview setting too. Many candidates don't listen carefully; instead, they merely use the interview questions as a point of departure to ramble on about themselves, and they offer answers to questions they haven't been asked. Fortunately for us introverts, we tend to spend more time listening than talking. Use your listening skills to your advantage by tuning in to the question, the questioner, and whatever you hear between the lines. Doing so will set you apart from the rest of the crowd.

"I remember an interview I had for a job," says Doug Fidoten, president of Dentsu America, Inc., a full-service advertising and marketing-communications company. "I had already met with a number of other executives, and this was the last one. The executive I met with looked at my résumé and initially didn't say anything. Many people would have nervously tried to fill the space. Maybe it was my introverted character, but I didn't. Eventually, the executive asked me questions, and we started a dialogue. The next day I was told that I got the job and that I had done particularly well with this executive. Maybe it was a stroke of luck. But maybe also it was the first bit of insight into what it meant to be an active listener."

Asking strong open-ended questions goes hand-in-hand with listening well. In Chapter 5, we covered the importance of asking open-ended questions in the context of networking. By doing so on interviews, you'll elicit more information from the interviewer. *Don't* just "get interviewed." *Do* prepare questions that demonstrate that you've done your homework and are abreast of the key issues facing the profession, the organization, the industry, and the interviewer. You'll also stand to learn quite a bit from the answers—notice the interviewer's verbal and nonverbal responses to your questions.

Describe What Contributions You Can Make

If you remember nothing else: Gear your elevator pitch, or the snappy description of who you are that we covered in Chapter 5, to the organization you're applying to. This will quickly establish who you are and what you have to offer your prospective employer.

Another must-do: You may have been a top performer throughout your career, and maybe you recently conquered the world. I'm sure your former employers would sing your praises. However, let's not forget the programming on my favorite radio station, WIIFM—except now *you'll* need to answer "What's in it for me?" from the standpoint of the hiring manager. What are you going to do to make her or his life easier? How will you make the organization you're applying to better? Rather than getting caught off-guard when you're asked what contributions you can make, why not have some sound bites polished and ready to go?

Write the elevator pitch you drafted in Chapter 5 in the space that follows. The process of writing it over again may help you see your elevator pitch differently—and you may even see where it needs tweaking. Imagine delivering this pitch at your dream organization, where you would have plenty of private space to gather your thoughts, fascinating projects that will enable you to make your imprint on society, friendly but noninvasive colleagues who don't need a lot of meetings (with you, anyhow!), and a short commute from home . . . or whatever it is that would delight you.

Your elevator pitch:

_____

_____

Before you can get the offer, however, you first must address the one problem your interviewer is most interested in solving by hiring you. If you're not sure, do some digging—use your imagination as well as your skills at inquiring and investigating. Write that problem in the space that follows, and then adjust your pitch to each specific interviewer.

The one problem the interviewer is most interested in your solving:

_____

_____

Your elevator pitch adjusted to address the problem you just described:

_____

_____

HOW TO PREPARE

Interviews can be miserable for the unprepared introvert, since we're at our best when we gather our thoughts before we speak. On the other hand, interviews can be extremely satisfying for those of us who thrive on digging around for market intelligence, gearing up for all kinds of questions, and polishing our pitch. The most satisfying part of going on interviews for me has always been the feeling of accomplishment I get when I've given it my best, regardless of the outcome. While some things have always been out of my control—like the emergence of an internal shoo-in candidate—when I've prepared well, I've usually gotten the offer. Same goes for many of my introverted coaching clients.

As part of your preparation, factor in plenty of time for mass-transit delays, coffee spills, and pantyhose snags. Cathie Black, president of Hearst Magazines, says: "Arrive 15 minutes early. Plan to check in at the building, since security can take a while. Go to the restroom and check your appearance. When you finally get to the interviewer's floor, cubicle, or office, you're not rushing. Even if you're nervous, it's okay, because you're excited about the appointment. If you come flying in five minutes late, it will rattle your confidence. I really don't care about somebody's being stuck in a traffic jam or being stopped by security. Remember: You don't have a second chance to make a good first impression."

A study at the Massachusetts Institute of Technology (MIT) underscores Black's advice: "Decades of research in social psychology illustrate the surprising power of first impressions. From contexts as diverse as evaluating classroom teachers, selecting job applicants, or predicting the outcomes of court cases, human judgments made on the basis of just a 'thin slice' of observational data can be highly predictive of subsequent evaluations."[3] Here's more about how you can prepare for a great interview.

I asked one leader from the public sector and one from the private sector what to do when an interviewer puts you on the spot with a difficult question. Kathleen Waldron, Ph.D., president of Baruch College, recommends buying time: "You can use phrases that don't sound stupid to stall as you're collecting your thoughts. Introverts should learn phrases such as, 'Gee, Joe and I were talking about that yesterday. That's a very interesting question.' Or you repeat back the question and say, 'Do I understand your question correctly?' Your mind races along faster than your voice, so it gives you time to think of what you want to say without a long silence that looks bad."

Cathie Black of Hearst Magazines notes: "It's perfectly fine to say, 'No one has ever asked me that question before. Let me think about it. I want to answer it in a thoughtful way.' That gives you a chance to create an answer in your head while you're saying somewhat meaningless words."

You may have to walk a fine line between being authentic and offering answers that are politically savvy. When the interviewer asks you stickier questions about gaps in your employment, what your last boss would say about you, and why you left your last job, you may even have to dance deftly. While I never recommend lying or stretching the truth, I do recommend casting your accomplishments and the contributions you can make to the hiring organization in the best light possible.

Analyzing Your Audience

Spend much of your prep time assessing your audience—the interviewer, the interviewer's boss, the organization, its culture, its

Interview Intelligence Toolkit

What to Learn About	Kinds of Information: (e.g., affiliations, education, past organizations, cultural background, interests)	Sources of Information: (e.g., headhunters, recruiters, someone you know in the hiring organization, Web sites, blogs, newspapers, magazines, trade journals)	Your Findings
The interviewer			
The interviewer's boss			
The interviewer's boss's boss			
Your prospective colleagues (Who's on the team?)			
Other stakeholders			
Is this a new position?			
If not, why did the last person leave?			

	Sources of Information	Your Findings
Describe the organization's culture (e.g., competitive, collaborative)		
Its mission		
Its biggest competitors		
What the organization values most		
How its doing against its short- and long-term objectives		
Anything else		

management structure, its mission, and so on. Much of what we covered in Chapter 4 will be helpful. I've always found a stark contrast between interview candidates who are more like insiders, having gathered information and peered inside an organization before interviewing, and those who just wing it. So first, let's determine what kind of information you need to help you do well on the interview. In the preceding table, gather information about the stakeholders and the organization where you'll be interviewing. Fill in whatever information you already have, and determine what you still need to obtain.

What insights have you had by doing this exercise? Do you already know everything you need to know about the organization and its key players? How far along are you in your information gathering? What else do you need to learn, and by when?

Preparing Your Résumé

Since we like to think before expressing ourselves, writing is a smart way for us introverts to communicate. Whether you're writing your résumé, a cover letter, a sales pitch, speaker's notes for a presentation, or a thank you note, you can benefit from finding a quiet place, taking your time to go inward, and immersing yourself in this process. Unlike interacting on an interpersonal level, writing doesn't put you on the spot and allows you to go at your own pace—what a gift for an introvert! Of course, I encourage you to seek input from people you admire, particularly those who are senior to you in your field, to help you tune up your résumé until it sings your praises in just the right key.

While the résumé formats that are widely accepted in most U.S. business environments don't invite much variety or creativity, you can still make yours pop. The challenge is creating a dynamic snapshot of your entire work life in a tidy black-and-white dossier. The appropriate content in this brief and formal document usually boils down to your contact information, work experience, education, and affiliations.

My advice: Stick to the basics. Include an objective, a list of key qualifications, and/or an executive summary on your résumé—along with lots of action verbs and keywords that will get picked up electronically by recruiters. Also highlight plenty of your accomplishments—what you did that benefited your employers in a concrete way. In most cases, you'll want to organize the contents of your résumé chronologically. An alternative and less commonly used format, however, is that of a functional résumé, which enables you to emphasize the experience you've had that's relevant to the organization you're applying to. This format is sometimes used by people in career transitions to showcase their transferable skills.

When I was looking to hire staff during my corporate days, I often got a stack of at least 50 résumés for a single job. Even though many of the candidates had already been prescreened by recruiters, I would glance at each résumé for 10 to 15 seconds and then put it in the "yes," "maybe," or "no" pile. Only 3 to 5 résumés would make it to the yes pile. Another 10 would go to the maybe pile. The rest went into the circular file. The yeses got the interviews. I invited the maybes only once I had met all the yeses and still needed more candidates. I have compared notes with colleagues and recruiters, and I've learned that my experience was common. So what do you need to do to consistently get to the yes pile? Consider the following:

■ **Highlight your accomplishments, not just your responsibilities.** As an introvert, this may be particularly challenging for you. Write not only a description of the jobs that you were required to do but also what you did that was above and beyond the call of duty. Also include the results—and the more you can quantify these facts, the better. Helpful resources can include your past performance reviews and graduate school applications. You can also contact former managers and colleagues who appreciated your contributions to get their input.

■ **Make it snappy.** Ask yourself if someone with a short attention span will get what you're good at and why she or he should hire you by glancing at your résumé. Then actually ask someone with a short attention span (Shhh!!!).

■ **Make it tight.** As a rough guideline, I recommend a one- to two-page résumé with plenty of "white space" around the text so that the layout doesn't look busy. Of course, in some fields, such as academia, a curriculum vitae, or CV, which enables you to offer a lengthier and more detailed list of what you've published or performed, is also commonly used. Regardless, err on the side of conciseness. You can share more during your interviews.

■ **Keep it simple and clean.**   Use only one or two fonts and a simple format. If you're not sure, check online resources such as www.monster.com and owl.english.purdue.edu for guidance. You can also use templates, such as the ones available on Microsoft Word, to guide you.

■ **Make it easy for the people screening your résumé to understand that you've got what it takes.**   Write an objective that jibes with the description of the job you're applying for. Or, if you prefer, write an executive summary offering an overview of your qualifications. However, don't make it just about you and how you're looking to be challenged or want to increase your knowledge. Tie it closely to what the organization is looking for, and focus on how the organization will benefit.

Of course, there's not one ideal résumé. I like the popular idea of creating different versions for different positions and organizations—as long as everything you say is accurate. So if you're an interior designer who has a little experience as a pastry chef, create a separate résumé to send to restaurants where you want to bake. Your pastry chef résumé would have to convince the hiring manager that you're a strong contender for the job. So it would have to highlight your relevant experience and perhaps include your experience as an interior designer as secondary information, for background only.

Remember that a résumé is a marketing document in which you can really shine—particularly as an introvert willing to dedicate the thought and time to word-smithing and polishing it. Of course, even polishing has its limits. I've worked with numerous clients who came to me with résumés worthy of framing. Be mindful of when it's time to shift your attention from adding more gloss to an already stellar résumé that will mostly be skimmed by hiring managers to getting out there and drumming up more interviews.

One more thing: Since résumés are often submitted electronically, your interview may be the only chance you'll have to offer the interviewer a hard copy. "Even if you've already sent it, don't assume that the interviewer has the five minutes to look at your résumé before you walk in the door," says Cathie Black. "Put it across the table so it's facing the interviewer and say, 'Just in case you need another copy of my résumé.'" To that end, make your résumé consistent with your appearance in your best interview outfit. In other words, print it on high-quality paper stock. Choose one in white or ivory, unless you're applying for a position in a design field, in which case you can probably express yourself more vividly. It should be completely smooth and clean, as if it were a museum-quality print.

Role-Playing and Mock Interviews

One of my favorite ways to prepare for an interview is to practice answering interview questions, many of which can be anticipated. Your answers will probably sound a lot different out loud than in your head. Practice with someone who is more supportive of than competitive with you and who has experience as an interviewer. However, if no one comes to mind, you can probably benefit from working with anyone you trust, even if just to have a witness and practice partner.

While you may be conditioned to seek brutally honest feedback, I'd like to offer another perspective: You probably already have a reasonably experienced inner critic to nag at you. Why not ask for the type of feedback that you want? For example, if you would feel flooded by hearing every little thing you did imperfectly, then specify before you start that you would just like to focus on one aspect of your interviewing technique—say, your body language.

Share a list of criteria (e.g., good eye contact, firm handshake, natural hand gestures) upon which you'd like to be evaluated. Ask your practice partner to videotape or audiotape your mock interviews. While it can take getting used to, seeing or hearing a recording of yourself is a great learning tool—and it may even build your confidence about your interview persona. Since, as an introvert, you are well suited to going inward and reflecting, you can take a close look at your performance, analyze it, and refine it.

HOW TO COMMUNICATE WITHOUT WORDS

Since you'll probably be seated during your interview, your nonverbal communication is mainly manifest in your posture, facial expressions, and hand and leg movements. I'll share the scoop on each of these and more, and you can rate your own performance. "Work on your self-confidence, which is an important part of success," says Cathie Black. "When you have something to say, people will listen. They're not going to listen if you're meek and if your body language is not giving off a sense of 'I know what I'm talking about.'"

Chances are you're not even aware of how you come across nonverbally. However, the process of rating yourself will help you increase your awareness. Rate yourself on a scale of 1 to 5 (1 = need significant improvement; 2 = need improvement; 3 = satisfactory; 4 = very good; and 5 = excellent) on each of the following. Then jot down one specific action (e.g., read a book on business etiquette; practice speaking while gesturing for five minutes a day in front of a mirror) you can take to get to the next level.

Handshake

It's one of the few socially acceptable instances when people in business touch each other, and it can have a profound effect on the first impression we make. I often think of candidates' limp-fish, tight-squeeze-grip, and slippery handshakes before I think of their other attributes for a long time to come. Memorable handshakes usually aren't good ones. How do you ensure that yours is firm but not crushing? Try it out on a few businesspeople you trust who would be willing to give you feedback on your handshake. If you get sweaty palms, remember to blot them privately just before hand-shake time. If you get the same constructive feedback more than once, consider adjusting your handshake and trying again; once you get it right, practice until it becomes second nature. Before an inter-view, remind yourself what you need to do differently.

Your self-assessment: _____

What you can do to get to the next level: _____

Where to Sit

If you're given a choice of where to sit, consider the following: What are you most comfortable facing? Avoid facing a window if the view—the people passing by or the bright light streaming in—would be distracting. I like to take a seat deep into a room so that if someone else enters, she or he won't pass behind me. You may have to decide whether to sit on a chair or a couch. If you find it awkward to sit side by side with the interviewer, which might give you less personal space and expose your notes, then choose a chair. If you're in a glass-walled conference room, consider sit-ting with your back to the bulk of the passer-by traffic to avoid feeling exposed. While you may consider other factors as well, make active choices that are both appropriate and best serve your needs.

Your self-assessment: _____

What you can do to get to the next level: _____

Posture

The biggest posture pitfall I see is candidates slumping in their seats or leaning back, sometimes with their feet extended in front of them, rather than sitting up straight and even leaning forward a bit to show interest. Practice answering some interview questions in a seated position with a book on your head, and you'll be unlikely to slouch.

Your self-assessment: _____

What you can do to get to the next level: _____

Facial Expressions

Be mindful of what you're saying with your facial expressions and whether they're consistent with the rest of your body language and your words. I recently interviewed an MBA student at a top graduate business school where I conduct mock behavioral interviews. She was dressed impeccably and was highly articulate; however, with her eyes averted and her face expressionless, she looked "shut down." Think of an aspect of the opportunity that excites you, and show it not only in your responses to the interview questions but also in your facial expressions.

A quick aside: There's a big difference between a real, or Duchenne, smile and a forced grin. The former is named after the nineteenth-century French neurologist Guillaume Duchenne, who determined that smiles reflecting genuine happiness used the muscles of both the mouth and the eyes—forming crow's feet. It's more attractive than it sounds, and besides, it's authentic. It might even given you a surprise boost. Go Duchenne!

Your self-assessment: _____

What you can do to get to the next level: _____

Hand Gestures

Use your hands naturally, as if you were speaking to a friend over coffee, to emphasize your points. The biggest mistake that candidates make is fidgeting. Avoid touching your hands or face, and don't twiddle a pen or other object. In the other extreme, occasionally candidates, in effect, sit on their hands. Some are so concerned about gesticulating grandly that they overcompensate by looking wooden. What do you do with your hands when you're listening? A simple and effective position is to rest them, relaxed, on the table in front of you; if there's no table, place your hands on the armrest of the chair or on your lap.

Your self-assessment: _____

What you can do to get to the next level: _____

Foot and Leg Movements

Since you'll probably be seated, be mindful of what you do with your legs and feet. A good default position is to firmly plant both feet on the floor straight beneath you. If you're more comfortable crossing your legs, then do so. However, err on the side of being still rather than nervously bouncing a foot on the floor or swinging your legs and risking kicking the interviewer!

Your self-assessment: _____

What you can do to get to the next level: _____

Interviewing over a Meal

The game intensifies when you interview over a meal. Choose food that isn't messy and requires minimal chewing, so you'll be free to speak without your mouth full. It may help to decide what you'll order in advance. Of course, avoid ordering alcohol, which could relax your inhibitions too much. Read up on table-manner etiquette to refresh your knowledge on the fine points of which fork to use, and so on.

Your self-assessment: _____

What you can do to get to the next level: _____

What to Have Ready

"All of us have seen shocking things when somebody comes for an interview," says Cathie Black. "I laugh about it in my book *Basic Black*. I might say, 'Here, take some notes,' and the candidate flimflams around in her pocketbook because she can't find a pen or she has a ratty little piece of paper."

Argh, I know that's been me. Now when I'm meeting with a prospective client, I put everything I'll need in an easily accessible inner pouch inside my portfolio bag. The pouch will contain a pen, a trim pad of paper, my PDA, and my business-card holder. This addresses my worst fear of having to empty out the contents of my purse! Enough about me.

Your self-assessment: _____

What you can do to get to the next level: _____

How You Sound

Does the quality of your voice help or hinder your ability to communicate? If it's hard for you to project, enunciate, or control the tone or some other aspect of your voice, I strongly recommend vocal training. It can take you a long way toward developing a more powerful, resonant voice, and it doesn't take forever. "If I have to strain to hear someone, I give up because it's too much of an effort," says Janet Riesel at Ernst & Young. Here's one quick vocal tip that has helped many of my clients and students: Avoid dropping the volume at the ends of your sentences. You'll sound so much more confident when you speak in a strong voice, clearly projecting every word in each sentence, rather than allowing your voice to trail off.

Your self-assessment: _____

What you can do to get to the next level: _____

Responding to Tough Questions on the Spot

As an introvert, I've always found that the most difficult aspect of being interviewed was answering tough questions on the spot. With no time to think, I'd forget to breathe. When I'd forget to breathe, my voice would go up an octave. With less oxygen going to my brain, the resulting thoughts were shallow and weak. The best thing you can do to avoid that quasi-scientific downward spiral is to anticipate the toughest questions. Of course, they're inevitable. So what do you do?

Your self-assessment: _____

What you can do to get to the next level: _____

HOW TO ANSWER THE TOUGHEST QUESTIONS

Interviewers will ask you about your weaknesses, your failures, and your character flaws. They'll pose questions with no reasonable answers. Janet Riesel of Ernst & Young shares a question she once heard: "'How many hotels are in the United States?' I'm sure there's a right answer, but interviewers usually want to see that the candidates know how to think and how they arrive at their answers." It's your responsibility to be unflappable, even while the interviewers are judging you and critiquing your every word.

So what about the answer to that gnawing question about your weaknesses? Headhunter Penny Doskow advises: "Don't say, 'I work too hard.' Offer more substance and put a positive spin on your strengths, such as: 'I get impatient when managers pit members of their team against each other. Instead, I create an environment in which each team member is an important cog in the wheel, and everyone's contributions matter toward the team's deliverable.'" Riesel adds, "I like to hear the candidate's self-improvement goals for the year and what he or she would like to do better. For example, every candidate can develop better computer skills or become a better public speaker. After all, we don't hire perfect people."

When I ask how to best answer the question "What is your biggest regret?" Riesel says: "I always appreciate when people say they tried a specific career because they thought it would be great or interesting, but when it didn't work out, they learned from it and went on to do something else. I prefer those candidates to those who say, 'I always wanted to go into my own business but never did.' I like it when people learn from their mistakes—at least they tried something they were initially passionate about."

While you can practice and practice your answers to some of these challenging questions, Riesel makes another important point: "Interviewers don't like to hear rehearsed answers that sound robotic. Instead, take a moment to think and compose your answers thoughtfully." So even if you have rehearsed, take a deep breath, and then tailor your answers to your audience.

In the space that follows, write three of the toughest questions you could be asked during an interview, and then write your answers. Practice out loud until you're satisfied with how you sound. Polish your content and delivery with a friend, colleague, or coach who can offer you valuable feedback.

1. Tough question:

_____

_____

Answer:

_____

_____

2. Tough question:

_____

_____

Answer:

_____

_____

3. Tough question:

_____

_____

Answer:

_____

_____

HOW TO DRESS TO IMPRESS

You may have heard the common wisdom that if you want to make good money, then look expensive. While you may regard designer clothing, a good haircut, and snappy shoes as window dressing, think of all the other windows that your interviewer will look at. If you're on par with another candidate in every other way and your appearance is sharper, more current, and more appropriate to the organization, you'll have an edge. You don't have to be flashy or slick. Instead, think about the type of image you'd like to project. How can you make your outward appearance reflect your inner richness? And what can you wear that will help you exude confidence?

If you're not sure what's appropriate to wear on an upcoming interview, find out. While wearing a suit is appropriate in many settings, it can increase your visibility in an undesirable way if it's out of place (e.g., an interview for a software engineering job).

While you might argue that you could probably squeak by in your lucky suit from the '90s, that you wouldn't want to work at an organization that would hire or disqualify you because of your appearance, or that some of the most successful people in the world are badly dressed billionaires, why handicap yourself? Ask someone you know in the organization, the recruiter, or the department's assistant about the dress code. In some cases you can also look on the Internet (e.g., Google Images) to find photographs of the leaders and employees of the organization to get a sense of how they put themselves together.

So it's interview day and you're ready. "Ask yourself, 'How do I look?'" says Cathie Black. "You'll feel better about yourself if you've got a nice outfit on." If you think that, as a card-carrying introvert, you don't want to draw attention to yourself, think again. Remind yourself of your end goal. We're looking to raise your visibility so you can make greater contributions to your organization and society. Do you want the job, the promotion, the raise, or the sale? Then look the part. "Some of this sounds superficial; however, it's true," says Black. "We judge people. You don't always have a chance to come back for a third, fourth, and fifth try."

What's Your Style?

If a successful leader in your field were to describe the style of your appearance (i.e., clothing, accessories, hair, grooming) to a colleague, whom might she or he compare you to? Are you more Michelle Obama or Laura Bush? Michael Douglas in *Wall Street* or Jack Klugman in *The Odd Couple*?

Whose image does your own resemble? (Name someone you know, a celebrity, or a fictional character.)

_____

Whose image do you aspire to?

_____

What will you do to adjust your current style to fit that image? When will you do it?

_____

_____

Who is a good person to witness and support you in this goal?

_____

I'm not assuming that just because you're an introvert your look is poorly coordinated or dated. On the contrary, you may put yourself together straight from the pages of your favorite fashion magazine, with touches of your own signature style. However, if you're so used to being invisible that you forget that people notice how you look, or if your head has been so buried in the books that you haven't looked up at a mirror lately, the following is for you.

You may prefer to blend in and not draw attention to yourself. That's fine, as long as you can accept it when a less qualified but more memorable candidate gets the job. Or when no one recognizes you for your ideas and talents, and you get passed up for promotions. How about a new approach? After all, didn't you pick up this book to get the recognition you deserve?

If you can't afford to buy the latest from Gucci, you can still look the part for less. Consider working with a personal shopper at a department store who can help you select outfits, hiring a personal image consultant, or buying designer clothes on eBay and at discount retailers, consignment stores, or outlets. Leaf through magazines to find a good look for you and to help focus your shopping efforts.

One last thought: Dressing the role means not only paying attention to the appropriateness of what you wear but also to the colors and fit that flatter you. I recently met a woman at a conference, and when we compared notes, we thought we knew the same colleague. Since he had a common name, the woman described him: "Isn't he the very tall, very thin, blue-eyed professor whose pants are always too short?" Yes, we realized it was unmistakably the same professor. I'm sure you don't want to be described that way. Likewise for the following fashion and style faux pas—at least, they'd be considered as such in many work environments—I've encountered as an interviewer:

- Scuffed shoes
- Clothing too large, too small, or ill fitting
- Outfits that look dated
- Too-short skirt
- Low-cut blouse
- Rumpled anything
- Bulging handbag or briefcase
- Overstuffed pockets
- Knapsack
- Shopping bags
- Hats indoors (except religious headwear)
- Flip-flops (unless you're working by a pool!)
- Bland colors that make the wearer look washed out
- Distracting colors and patterns
- Crooked or outdated eyeglass frames
- Belly hanging over belt
- Color-treated hair with roots showing
- Men's tie of an outdated width, length, or design

Grooming

Here are a few quick words about grooming basics. Skip this section if you're already impeccable in this department. If not, address whatever you need to tune up. Make sure:

- Your teeth are flossed and show no signs of what you had for lunch (likewise, your breath).

- Your fingernails are trimmed and clean. I'm amazed at how many people have a blind spot for dirt beneath their fingernails.
- Your clothing is free of wrinkles, lint, and dog and cat hair.
- Your hairstyle is current. If not, get a good haircut. Check the style pages of fashion magazines to be sure. Men: Your own hair, even if it's thinning or receding, is more attractive than a hairpiece.
- You go easy on perfume or aftershave because many scents repel some people and make others sneeze.
- (For women only) You know how to apply makeup in a flattering way; if you're unsure, find tips in beauty magazines or invest in a session with a makeup artist.
- (For men only) The amount and style of your facial hair (your beard, moustache, or goatee) are appropriate to the work environment, your religious observance notwithstanding.

Packing Your Bag

When I'm getting ready to go to a meeting of any kind, I schedule time to pack my bag. Sometimes I even lay out everything I'll need for the next day the night before. By making this its own step in my planning process, I don't forget anything important and I arrive feeling ready. Here's a checklist of items you might bring for a job interview:

_____ Résumé (several copies)
_____ Portfolio or briefcase
_____ Business cards
_____ Pen
_____ Notepad
_____ Wristwatch
_____ Small cough drops
_____ Handkerchief or tissues
_____ Shoe cloth

_____ Umbrella
_____ Eye drops
_____ Reading glasses
_____ (For women only) Extra pantyhose, cosmetics
_____ (For men only) Extra tie
_____ Other: _____

HOW TO FOLLOW UP

You've made it through the steeplechase and high jumps of the e-mail, phone, and in-person screenings. Assuming all went well, soon you'll either be invited for more interviews, or you'll get an offer and discuss compensation. But first, how do you follow up on your interviews?

The simple answer is by sending to each person you met a thoughtfully crafted thank you note. I included sample wording for a thank you note following an informational interview in Chapter 5. Use the same idea when writing a thank you note after a job interview. The main difference is that you'll include a line about how you can make a significant contribution to the hiring organization. Make the whole thing a few snappy sentences long, and send it by mail or e-mail, depending on what's more appropriate. Regardless, I'm a fan of the 24-hour rule: Don't wait longer to send it.

Besides writing, what else can you do? The quick answer is, "It depends." If you've been told not to call the employer, then don't. If a headhunter or other contact introduced you to your interviewer, it's probably more appropriate to follow up with that person. It's a delicate balance between showing interest and appearing too eager. The best piece of advice I can offer is to ask the interviewer her or his preference toward the end of the interview; also ask if it would be better to follow up by e-mail or phone.

HOW TO NEGOTIATE COMPENSATION

Now for one of the most emotionally charged aspects of the interview process: commanding your worth in the market. "Ascertain your value to the other party and demonstrate it regularly to them—not just when you're negotiating," says Pamela Wheeler, director of operations for the Women's National Basketball Players Association (WNBPA). This fundamental piece of advice often eludes so many of us.

Show Empathy

While you may think of negotiating as a tug-of-war, showing empathy for the other party's concerns can actually go a long way. The hiring manager probably has a budget to manage, and she may have a ceiling on how much she can offer you before she has to obtain special approval from her boss, the board of directors, and so on. You can demonstrate your empathy by verbally acknowledging her concerns.

Alex (Sandy) Pentland, Ph.D., describes a surprising way to show empathy—through mimicry—in his book *Honest Signals*, which is based on research from MIT. He describes mimicry as "the copying of smiles, interjections, and head nodding during a conversation." He also notes: "In both salary negotiations and sales, we have seen that mimicry functions as an honest and effective signal of the trust as well as the empathy required for successful negotiations and financial transactions. What is particularly impressive is the effectiveness of this honest signal: unconscious, automatic mimicry improved financial results by *20 to 30 percent*."[4]

It's not clear to what extent conscious mimicry would yield the same results. However, as Pentland also notes: "It is hard to consciously fake these signals, thereby falsely communicating your attitude or intention. Method acting does appear to work, however, if you really, fully put yourself into a particular social role. Whether it is as the leader, the team member, or another role, we find that your signaling automatically and unconsciously changes to match. The fact that you can mentally 'put on' different social roles and have your signaling follow suit means that we can change our unconscious communications." Could this be a scientific basis for the advice to "fake it until you make it"?

Use Your Strengths as an Introvert

Use your introverted strengths at research and information gathering to learn how much someone with your level of experience, skills, and education is typically paid for a given position. How do you find this out? Look to your professional network to get connected to people "in the know." Talk to recruiters, headhunters, colleagues, and contacts in professional organizations, and read job listings as well as the latest articles and blogs in newspapers. Also check online resources (e.g., Salary.com and the Bureau of Labor Statistics at www.bls.gov). While it takes some sleuthing, you should be able to determine a realistic range.

You can also learn the reputations and employee ratings of various organizations at resources like Glassdoor.com. Some companies are known to compensate their employees well; others offer low salaries but ample bonuses or stock options, or excellent health benefits. Also, consider that salary ranges for specific positions differ by country and region.

While we're on the topic of compensation, a survey by the Society for Human Resource Management (SHRM) found that employees attributed their job satisfaction to the following criteria, in the order of importance: employees' perception of job security, benefits, compensation, feeling safe in the workplace, communication between employees and senior management, and opportunities to use skills and abilities. So compensation was ranked number 3; however, it ranked number 1 among employees 35 and younger.[5]

If compensation is high on your list, here are some tips to help you negotiate a favorable package:

■ **Remember your strengths.** I've heard too many of my introverted clients say to me that they're lousy negotiators, resigning themselves before even trying. If that's you, take stock of what would make you a strong negotiator, such as your abilities to research, listen actively, and think deeply. Most of us aren't born negotiators; however, negotiating is a skill that we can learn to hone with some practice.

■ **Be mindful of your negotiating style.** Just as we may have a not-so-flattering picture of a salesperson in our mind's eye, some of us imagine that only a blowhard "wins" at negotiations. What's your style? Do you tend to compete, accommodate, avoid, or compromise? If you're competitive, make a commitment to pay attention to the other party's needs. If you tend to readily accommodate, stay attuned to your own needs so you don't sell yourself short. If you typically avoid conflict, remember that you probably won't get what you want unless you engage. If you compromise readily, reach for a better solution in which both parties can fully, rather than partially, win.

■ **Research like crazy.** As we discussed earlier, find out as much as you can about the pay structure at the organization you're considering and within other organizations in the field. Find out about turnover rates. Do people stick around, or do they typically leave to get bigger bumps in their compensation?

■ **Prepare and rehearse for the toughest aspects.** Role-play the hardest parts with someone you trust. Ask for constructive feedback.

■ **Don't rush to discuss pay.** While you may already have a sense of the pay structure before you start the interview process, it's probably best to hold off on discussing pay until you sense that the employer is truly sold on you. Otherwise, there's nothing to negotiate, and you may get disappointed by having played your cards too soon. One caveat: It would be a shame to waste your time interviewing only to find out after a monthlong process that the pay is half of what you expected. Try to find out the salary and/or compensation range before you enter the interview process. Once the employer makes an offer, it's probably time to negotiate your compensation.

■ **Ask open-ended questions to find out more information.** Invite the other party to share more information by asking *who*, *what*, *where*, *when*, *why*, and *how*, rather than yes-or-no questions. Here are examples of the types of questions you might ask, depending on the situation:

— Who is responsible for decisions about compensation? (It's a good idea to know who all the players are; there may be some behind the scenes who aren't coming to the negotiating table.)

— How does the organization compensate its employees? (What are the base salary, bonus, options, revenue-sharing, and benefit packages?)

— What is the salary range for someone in this position? How about the position one level higher?

— If the job is in the for-profit world, what is a typical sign-on bonus for someone in this type of position at the company?

— What is the average compensation increase each year for this type of position?

— What benefits are included in addition to the compensation package? (While the compensation may fall short of your expectations, it may be possible to negotiate an extra week of vacation, telecommuting, a variable work schedule, or something else you value. See the section that follows, titled "Negotiate Nonsalary Items Too.")

— What are the promotion opportunities, and how have they played out in the past for this type of position?

■ **Always have a clear alternative strategy in case negotiations reach an impasse.** What happens if the negotiations don't go your way, if the offer gets rescinded, or if the organization offers you only a fraction of your worth? Always be clear about your "best alternative to a negotiated agreement" (BATNA), as developed by negotiation researchers Roger Fisher and Bill Ury of the Harvard Program on Negotiation.[6] Your BATNA, or in essence your Plan B, is what would happen if you were to walk away from a negotiation.

■ **Once you're at the negotiating table, listen carefully for the other party's needs.** It's easy to get tunnel vision in pursuit of the numbers you have in mind. Paraphrase what the other party says so that you both are clear that you're listening.

■ **Offer a vision of a mutually positive outcome for you, the hiring manager, and the organization.** This transcends the potential haggling aspect of negotiations. When the other party is sold on bringing you on board, she or he will more likely be your champion, and the dynamic will be quite different from that of two parties quibbling over the price of a used car.

■ **Treat the negotiation as a collaboration rather than a competition.** By showing genuine interest in the needs of the other party and enthusiasm at the prospect of working together, you're inviting your goodwill to be reciprocated.

■ **If the other party says the compensation is not negotiable and you're still interested, explore your options.** Discuss the possibility of short-term employment, followed by performance and salary reviews.

■ **Show appreciation to the other party.** Negotiating is hard work. It's also an opportunity to lay the foundation for a strong working relationship. How each party approaches this challenging communication says volumes about both of you. Start on the right foot by allowing the negotiation to move the relationship forward, rather than creating a stumbling block you'd be happy to forget.

■ **Honor your introverted need to think about things before commenting.** Avoid agreeing to a compensation package on the spot. It's usually best to at least sleep on an offer. When you further consider the prospective agreement and discuss it with a few trusted friends and colleagues, you may come up with new angles to explore. Thank the other party for the offer she's made. Then say you'd like to think about it for a day (or two) and that you'll follow up by a specific date.

■ **Think about what the other party has at stake.** After all, if the hiring manager doesn't play his cards right, he stands to lose a valuable asset: You! It can be a drain on his time and resources if your negotiations fall through and he either has to start over with his second-choice candidate or conduct an entirely new search.

■ **Always be calm and grounded.** Even when the negotiations get tough, act as clearly, confidently, and true to yourself as possible, and don't let your emotions get in the way. Also remember that you speak with more than your words. Be conscious of your posture, eye contact, hand gestures, and facial expressions, and pay close attention to what the other party is telling you nonverbally.

■ **Get it in writing.** I've heard too many war stories about handshake agreements gone bad. Even when you and the other party trust each other, so much can undermine your agreement. The hiring manager could leave the organization and you could get stuck with a miserly new boss. Or you could remember the terms of the agreement differently from the hiring manager. Or a new cost-cutting initiative could put a freeze on increases, bonuses, and promotions. Don't leave yourself vulnerable. Get an employment contract, or at the very least an e-mail, from the hiring manager or someone in the human resources department confirming the compensation package you agreed to. If all else fails, write the e-mail yourself and request a response from the organization.

Getting the Compensation You Deserve

Susan Cain, author of *Quiet: The Power of Introverts in a World That Can't Stop Talking* (to be published in 2011) and president of The Negotiation Company, shares an anecdote about how she helped one of her clients ace a salary negotiation:

I had an elegant and self-assured client who was preparing for an interview for a director of business affairs position. She had great work experience but didn't have an MBA. In typical introvert fashion, she was fixated on what she lacked rather than on all the essential skills she could bring to the company.

The first thing we had to do was a mind-shift, at a gut level, to the point at which she believed that she was an asset to the company. MBA, shmem-B-A! We practiced how she would respond to interview questions that could arise. She wanted to acknowledge that she didn't have an MBA and explain why it didn't matter without sounding defensive. This was another invaluable introvert's strength: She was willing to prepare ad nauseum, to the point at which you'd never have known that she was nervous about the question.

We also prepared how she would ask for a higher salary than the opening offer. Here we ran into another introvert's strength. She was so gracious and understated in her self-presentation that she was able to take quite an assertive position. She asked for a lot more money without coming across as aggressive. She ended up with a starting salary of $15,000 more than the company initially offered her. And she earned the respect of the CEO, who told her that when he saw how well she negotiated for herself, he knew that she would negotiate that way on behalf of the company, and they actually wanted her at "any" price.

Negotiate Nonsalary Items Too

Keep in mind the following items you can negotiate whenever appropriate, according to Susan Cain:

- Flextime
- Work-at-home options
- Stock options
- Contract
- Moving expenses
- Cost-of-living adjustment
- A raise in the future, based on achieving certain agreed-upon objectives
- Resources to do the job (additional staff, increased budget, expense account, training)
- Whom you'll report to
- Health benefits
- Life insurance
- Title
- Promotion based on a certain milestone
- Bonus or other incentives
- Starting bonus
- Starting date
- Office space
- Vacation
- Personal and sick days
- Commuting costs
- Parking costs
- Car or car allowance
- Club memberships

So what do you do when the style of your negotiating partner is "my way or the highway"? You can deal with people who are confrontational in several ways. Lee E. Miller, author with Barbara

Jackson of *UP: Influence, Power, and the U Perspective: The Art of Getting What You Want*, offers two approaches: "You have to understand what I call the 'U perspective' of the other people. If they're all about winning, then let them win. Start from a place much further from where you want to end. This way, you can give up more without sacrificing what's important to you, and they feel like they're 'winning.'" Miller continues: "Another way is to ask people for help, as opposed to making them feel that they're in competition with you. Doing so short circuits the winner-loser dynamic." Of course, when you can't avoid people with aggressive negotiating styles, arm yourself with the facts, stay calm and grounded, and always have your BATNA lined up.

We've covered a lot of ground in this chapter. It's amazing how a job interview—a meeting that typically lasts just an hour—can have such a profound impact on determining the course of your career. If you do better by preparing, researching, and rehearsing before speaking, use these activities to your advantage. Whether you're already looking for a job or just starting to think about it, the most important thing to remember is that you have strengths as an introvert that you can put into action to land job offers.

In Chapter 8, you'll get some enlightening—and sometimes surprising—glimpses into how the other half thinks. We're often so immersed in our own inner worlds as introverts that we neglect to benefit from the perspectives of people who are different from us. So in the next chapter, you'll get to step outside yourself and into the shoes of extroverts. I've interviewed some highly successful, and even luminary, extroverts and introverts. I've spoken with the likes of Bill Clinton and Warren Buffett, who generously offered their viewpoints to help enrich the dialogue and understanding between the *I*s and *E*s of the world. This will further bolster your ability to promote yourself to introverts and extroverts alike.

REFLECTIONS AND ACTIONS

What You Learned

1. _____

   _____

2. _____

   _____

3. _____

   _____

Action: What will you do?	How You'll Do It: What support or further information will you obtain?	Accountability: Whom will you tell about this action?	Completion Date: By when?

eight

Your Opposite

The World According to Jo(e) Extrovert

Are you ready to commune with the other half of the world? While extroverts can learn plenty from us introverts, in this chapter we'll learn from extroverts—by observing them, talking to them, and considering their advice about self-promotion. Of course, it would exhaust us to do everything extroverts do to promote themselves; however, there's no law against taking a page or two from their playbook--and then doing things our way. Regardless of whether you consider yourself deeply introverted, wildly extroverted, or somewhere in between, this chapter can broaden your thinking by offering a variety of viewpoints about self-promotion through different lenses. We'll look at how introverts and extroverts can be alien to each other, and ultimately, we'll determine how we can promote ourselves in an extroverts' world.

COMMUNICATING WITH THE OTHER HALF

For Introverts Communicating with Extroverts

1. Be prepared to discuss a few light conversation topics as a way of connecting with your extroverted conversation partners.

2. Arrive at meetings well rested and refreshed to help prevent sensory overload.

3. Just as you prefer to think through your ideas before you talk about them, extroverts often like to work through their ideas out loud and bounce them off others. Expect to do some brainstorming at a meeting with extroverts.

4. While you may normally prefer to wait your turn to speak, be prepared to jump in when speaking at a meeting of extroverts.

5. Be patient with questions extroverts ask that seem invasive. Rather than critiquing their questions, just offer whatever you're comfortable sharing.

6. If you're stumped by a question, respond that you need a moment to think about it or that you'll follow up with an answer later.

7. Recognize extroverts' needs to have plenty of varied activities and people to talk to; an extrovert may be bored by an in-depth discussion behind closed doors with one person on a single topic.

8. Keep in mind that extroverts tend to be action oriented and they rely on the outside world for input and stimulation; balance that with your more inward focus.

9. Just as you may have deep knowledge about a few topics, appreciate extroverts' breadth of knowledge on many topics.

10. Avoid sending extroverts long e-mails or leaving detailed phone messages. (Many busy introverts will appreciate this too!) Extroverts may skim or only focus on the first few words.

11. Remember that while you're likely to have just a few close friends, extroverts like to know lots of people as acquaintances.

For Extroverts Communicating with Introverts

1. Welcome introverts to state our opinions, but avoid putting us on the spot. Distribute an agenda and ask for our input

privately, by e-mail, prior to a meeting to give us time to compose our thoughts.

2. Avoid asking introverts questions that we may experience as too personal or invasive; be patient with our need to get to know you over time.
3. Limit chitchat to the beginning of a conversation, and get to the more substantive parts more quickly.
4. Just as you may have a breadth of knowledge on many topics, appreciate introverts for our depth of knowledge about a few topics.
5. Make appointments with introverts rather than dropping by unannounced.
6. Respect introverts' need for private space. Do not stand too close during a conversation or reach into our space.
7. Remember that what you find stimulating (e.g., multitasking) may be overwhelming for introverts; many of us need to quietly focus on one thing at a time.
8. Consider meeting with your introverted colleagues in a quiet space to help ensure minimal interruptions. Do something more social before and after the meeting if you need more people time.
9. Give introverts time alone to do our best thinking and allow for sufficient breaks during meetings.
10. Recognize that introverts tend to undersell our accomplishments and potential contributions.
11. Let introverts finish speaking, count to three (to yourself!), and then speak; do not fill in the pauses.

AN INTROVERT'S DAREDEVIL MOTORCYCLE STUNT

To help encourage you to put yourself "out there," I repeatedly endured the introvert's equivalent of a daredevil motorcycle stunt. I mustered the courage to approach a few people who've achieved household-name status to get advice about visibility for you and to offer you inspiration. I met boxing promoter Don King outside a star-studded Upper East Side Italian restaurant, Craig Newmark of craigslist and marketing guru Seth Godin during their respective speaking engagements at New York University (NYU), Earvin "Magic" Johnson at Barnes & Noble, Leonard Nimoy at a talk he gave at the 92nd Street Y in New York, Chita Rivera after one of her shows, and former President Bill Clinton in a hotel lounge. At a Berkshire Hathaway annual meeting, I had the thrill of asking Warren Buffett a question whose answer I shared with you in Chapter 6. And I got the skinny on visibility from the extroverted media impresario and president of Hearst Magazines, Cathie Black. Vroom! I'll detail some of the more colorful encounters in this chapter.

Battleship

I'm at a favorite café, drafting this book on my laptop, while my boyfriend, Isaac, is by my side, working on one of his software development projects. A sporty looking Australian comes up to our table and says: "Excuse me. My friends and I were wondering what you were doing. We've seen you here for the past few nights. Are you playing Battleship?" Amused, Isaac and I tell him about our respective projects. When I mention my book for introverts, he says, "I guess I won't be needing that!" I respond that he must have some introverts in his life. "Yeah, they're sitting over there," he says, pointing to his table. To many extroverts, the idea of an enjoyable night out with one's partner wouldn't entail sitting next to each other while quietly working on separate projects. However, to Isaac and me, who are both introverts, it's a perfect evening. In fact, we position little Post-it flags on the top or sides of our laptops—in the style of an old taxi meter—to signal to one another when we're available to talk versus when we're deep in thought!

Of course, I don't mean to suggest that you should promote yourself by stopping celebrities on the street. Instead, I'd like to encourage you to think about where you want your career to go. If raising your visibility will help get you there, I'll help you do it in a way that's authentic to you. Whether that means quietly blogging, asking clients for their business, or dare I say launching a motorcycle over a few dozen tractor trailers, I'm right there with you. As always, we'll look inward before going outward— or upward!

A DAY IN THE LIFE OF JO(E) EXTROVERT

Julie Gilbert, who was a senior vice president at Best Buy Co., Inc., at the time of our interview, shares a glimpse into her typical work-day. Gilbert, who describes herself as "very extroverted," is currently the founder and principal of WOLF (Women's Leadership Forum) Means Business.

Julie Gilbert's Workday

Morning	"My phone's on 24 hours a day. It doesn't matter if it's 3:00 in the morning. I'm going to take the call, especially if it is someone who needs help in some way. I wake up by 5:00, and the first thing I do is check my BlackBerry to see who's been e-mailing me. Then I jump online and start responding. I get about 150 e-mails a day. I get on top of what I call 'red alert' e-mails. Very shortly thereafter, I work out at a local gym to stay in shape, think through the day, clear my head, and meet people—all at the same time." "I check my BlackBerry right when I get off the treadmill. In many cases, I'll check it while I'm running just to see what's cooking. While I'm driving to the office, I call back whoever called me while I was working out."

	"Then I get ready for my first meeting. I have meeting after meeting in the office when I'm there, and they're traditionally setting the vision for the organization. Between meetings, I'm calling people back, because the phone is ringing all day long." "I may be walking into a room of retail employees that are part-time and delivering a motivational speech on how we can win business and engage the insights of all employees in this pursuit—pulling insights out of them and getting them to engage in a dialogue. I hope they walk out feeling that they matter, that they had ideas, and that their voices were heard. I want them to feel that something may happen with their ideas because I linked them with other people in the room who could enable those ideas to come true."
Lunchtime	"Some people eat lunch in their office. I try to get out of the office and go to the company cafeteria or a restaurant that's close to work because I'm going to meet people while I'm there. I've got to eat anyway. So I grab a salad, sit at the bar. I don't sit at a table by myself. I just start talking to people around me because they're doing the same thing. And I meet people very, very quickly and make links to other people, other things. I go back to the office and again get through the meeting, meeting, meeting agenda." "One thing that I probably do differently: Instead of having one-on-one or even project meetings with three or four people in my office, I schedule those meetings at a local coffee shop inside our corporate headquarters. I want the work and the team to be visible—a lot of senior executives walk by. It's a great time for me to stop them and say, 'Shawn, how are you? What is happening in your area that I can help with? Do you know Shelly, Bethany, and Kim? They're doing amazing work. And, by the way, here are some of the outcomes they've gotten.' It can be a bit disruptive in terms of the content of the meeting, but the team members feel valued."

Evening	"In the evening, I'll do a lighter workout at the gym or even run around the lake, and when I'm doing that, I'm seeing people, meeting people. And then I'll have dinner with someone. It could be a customer that wants to meet me, so I'll take them out to dinner and really get to know them. Or I could be delivering a speech for an organization. I could be meeting with employees from my company who are in from out of town." "And then, as I'm driving home, I'm calling people back again. I get home and do a few e-mails. I get to then spend some quality time with the family and find out how they are doing and what happened in their day. And then it's lights out to another day."

How does Gilbert's day compare with yours? What does thinking about her day do for you? Inspire you? Exhaust you just reading about it? What's one thing you can learn from her?

ALIENS

Introverts and extroverts can be alien to each other. Still, it's not better to be one personality type over another. Being an extrovert doesn't mean that you're smarter or more talented than your introverted counterparts, and the opposite is true as well. Put an extrovert alone in a quiet room all day and she will crave people contact. Put an introvert in a quiet room, or, better yet, under a tree, and he's happy reading a book. Just as extroverts get energy from talking to lots of people, introverts would rather say less to fewer people.

Since you're probably already quite familiar with looking at life from an introvert's perspective, now let's take a closer look at the world according to Jo(e) Extrovert. The following tips will help you promote yourself to the more outward-facing half of the population, which generally thrives on interacting and doing more of

The Secret Handshake

I recently spoke at a conference for a professional organization of actuaries, a profession with a reputation for being a magnet for introverts. The joke that they all seemed to know was some variation on this: "How can you tell an introverted actuary from an extroverted one?" The punch line: "The extroverted actuary looks at the other actuary's shoes." I've also heard this time-worn joke applied to accountants. When I interviewed people for this book, because of the unfortunate social stigma tied to introversion, I never asked them directly whether they were introverts—although those who looked mostly at their own shoes offered some clues! Once we got to talking, however, many shared that they were indeed introverts, and then they reached across the table with the secret handshake.

A Great Pairing

I've often enjoyed working with extroverts, whose energy and style often complement my own. Doug Fidoten, president of Dentsu America, Inc., a full-service advertising and marketing-communications company, offers his own perspective: "There can be very interesting combinations in business life that just happen and they click. And you look back and say, 'Wow! That was a great pairing, a lot got done, and we were quite a team. How did that happen?' Often I've looked back and seen that the pairing happened to be an introvert and an extrovert and found that the chemistry was just right."

the talking. Of course, these tips may lead you to insights about promoting yourself to introverts as well. The key is to think about the preferences and interests of your stakeholders, and how you can best appeal to them.

Does it ever seem as if extroverts speak a language that's foreign to you? The following chart, which was contributed by Kathy Haff Lineker, breaks down the language barrier between introverts and extroverts.

Extrovert's versus Introvert's Lexicon

Word	Extrovert's Definition	Introvert's Definition
Alone, adj.	Lonely	Enjoy some peace and quiet
Book, n.	Doorstop Paperweight	Source of comfort Safe and inexpensive method of traveling, having adventures, and meeting interesting people
Bored, adj.	Not frantically busy	Stuck making small talk, and unable to escape politely
Free time, n.	A time when you do group activities (See Introvert's definition of *work*.)	A time when you read without interruption until you're in danger of going blind
Friend, n.	Someone who makes sure that you're never alone	Someone who understands that you're not rejecting her or him when you need to be alone
Good manners, n.	Making sure people aren't left all by themselves; filling in any silences in a conversation	Not bothering people unless it's necessary or they approach you (Sometimes you can bother people you know well, but make sure they aren't busy first.)
Home, n.	A place to invite everybody you know	A place to hide from everybody you know

Internet, n.	Another medium for advertising A place where geeks with no life hang out	A way to meet other introverts (You don't have to go out, and writing allows you to think before just blurting something out.)
Love, n.	Never having to do anything alone	Being understood and appreciated
Phone, n.	Lifeline to other people—your reason for living	Necessary (?) evil, and yet another interruption; occasionally useful, but mostly a nuisance
To go out, n.	Requires at least two people, and the more the better (Constant chatter, loud music, sports, and crowds are all fun components of going out.)	Can be done alone or with others; enjoyable if there's some point to it (i.e., in order to see a band, a movie, a play, or perhaps to have a stimulating discussion with one or two close friends)
Work, n.	Having to read, write, listen, or concentrate on anything	Being pestered every five minutes about something trivial and not being allowed to concentrate

JO(E) EXTROVERT'S NEEDS AND PET PEEVES

The premise is simple: by paying attention to the needs and pet peeves of your target audiences, your message will be more compelling to them. Conversely, if you ignore these valuable pieces of information, you can do more damage than good. For example, you could have given the best speech ever, but if you spoke for two hours without a break to a group of jet-lagged executives who just ate (and drank) lunch, how well do you think your speech was actually received? So at the risk of overgeneralizing—because we're all individuals—here are some typical needs and pet peeves of extroverts. I've left some space for you to add other needs and pet peeves of extroverts you've observed.

Jo(e) Extrovert's Needs

- Real-time people contact (e.g., in person, by phone)
- Frequent opportunities to meet new people
- An audience to appreciate her or his ideas, anecdotes, and jokes
- Constant activity and engagement
- Lots of people to call and visit
- Other: _____

Jo(e) Extrovert's Pet Peeves

- Too much alone time
- Receiving long, detailed e-mails
- Monotony, routine
- Feeling unwelcome when she or he drops by your space
- "Pulling teeth" to get introverts to express themselves
- Other: _____

Write your needs and pet peeves as an introvert in the space that follows.

Your (Introvert's) Needs

- _____
- _____
- _____
- _____
- _____

Your (Introvert's) Pet Peeves

- _____
- _____

- _____
- _____
- _____

Now that we've talked about Jo(e) Extrovert's needs and pet peeves and you've considered your own, what have you learned? As an introvert, one of my needs is lots of quiet time to process my thoughts. I do that much better alone or in conversation with one person—who listens!—than when interacting with multiple people, particularly a group of chatterboxes. This contrasts with Jo(e) Extrovert's need to, well, extrovert. How are your pet peeves different from Jo(e) Extrovert's? What do you have in common? What will you do differently to promote yourself to extroverts as a result? Reflect on your answers, and, in the space that follows, jot down one insight you gleaned from completing this exercise.

_____

_____

_____

HOW TO PROMOTE YOURSELF TO JO(E) EXTROVERT

I picture myself at the old Algonquin Roundtable with pundits from my circle, and we're discussing how introverts can promote themselves to Jo(e) Extrovert—who, incidentally, is busy working the room. Here's what the pundits say:

■ **Listen.** "Too many people misunderstand what the other person is saying," says Cathie Black, president of Hearst Magazines. "Speak slowly, have your points, go over them, and listen to what the other person says. It's not just listening to his voice. Watch his body language. If somebody shuts down, you'll see it on her face.

Thriving in an Extroverted World

Ken Frazier, executive vice president and president of Global Human Health at Merck & Co., Inc., shares his thoughts on how an introvert can thrive in an extroverted world. "You don't have to compete with the loudest person in the room. And if you do, then you're probably in the wrong situation. Find one setting where people are more discerning of the value rather than the volume of comments," he says. "You may have to develop a work persona that's different from your home persona. Practice it every day and be conscious of how you are around others. The same is true of extroverted people. They have to be conscious of how they are around others. Are they coming on too strong? Are they being overly verbose? Recognize and understand the signals you get from others, and then act on them." I ask Frazier how to do this. He replies: "Find peers who are willing to help you understand how you're coming across. Be open to responsible coaching from colleagues who care about you."

If she's looking at her BlackBerry or if she interrupts you 16 times, you've lost her. You can say things like, 'Maybe I ought to come back another time. You're obviously busy, busy, busy.'" Black concludes: "So communication is critical; it's the sum of the parts—and it's not just verbal."

■ **Interrupt.** I once heard an introvert say that she just wanted to get a pause in edgewise. While it might seem ironic to suggest that you interrupt right after I suggested that you listen, sometimes interrupting is appropriate, and even necessary. Michele Wucker, executive director of the World Policy Institute, tells how she handles her live appearances on national TV as an introvert: "The hardest thing was to learn to interrupt. You're expected to do it, and it's entertainment. I just decided that I was going to do it. I kept trying, and then all of a sudden it happened. I really started to enjoy my debates with Pat Buchanan when I could say, 'Wow! I got the last word in today.'"

■ **Jump back in when you've been interrupted.**   Extroverts like to talk, and they might even fill in your every pause. It may be a challenge to wedge in a word when talking to Jo(e) Extrovert. You can sit quietly at a meeting with a room full of extroverts, or you can choose to make yourself visible. "You really have to sometimes be firm and point out nicely when someone interrupts you. Smile and say, 'Why don't you let me finish this thought, and then you can go?' Or, 'I think it's my turn,'" says Kathleen Waldron, Ph.D., president of Baruch College, and an outgoing introvert. She adds that using a little humor can go a long way.

■ **Share what you're thinking.**   People can't see your mind at work, and you won't get credit for your thoughts if they remain in your head. "Introverts don't share all that they have available. Just spit it out. I often want to know more. Help me understand what you're thinking," says Michael Braunstein, ASA, MAAA, a very extroverted actuary at Aetna Inc. I met Braunstein at a big regional conference of actuaries, where he worked the room as if he were driving a fast convertible and somehow picking up more passengers at every turn.

■ **Give external signals.**   "As an extrovert, I look outward for cues about how to connect effectively with each person I meet," says Elizabeth Guilday, cofounder of the Professional Certificate in Coaching Program at NYU and president of Indigo Resources Inc. "Making a connection is important to me. So I'm especially attentive to demonstrating that I understand you, and I look for signals that you understand me. If I get a clear signal, then you've satisfied my extrovert's need."

■ **Show your face.**   While it may tax you to socialize too much, it's important to get out there and be seen. Be smart and strategic about how and where you spend your time. "You don't have to be the loudest talker and the greatest joke teller. Instead, you're the person who's always around and who provides information and contacts," says Shoya Zichy, the extroverted author (with Ann Bidou) of *Career Match*. Make an appearance, talk to a few key people, and then go home.

▪ **Position yourself as an expert.** Figure out how to make your knowledge invaluable to others. Get known as the "go-to" person for your area of expertise. Harness your introverted strengths, and write or deliver presentations on what you know that others don't to increase your visibility. "Say you're an expert in ferrets," says Howard Greenstein, social media strategist and president of the Harbrooke Group consultancy. "If you publish a ferret article a week for 52 weeks, before you know it, you're going to come up a lot higher when someone types 'ferret' into a search engine than if you just have a site that says, 'The Ferret Expert.'"

▪ **Succeed by filling existing needs.** "The first way to succeed is to produce and do a lot of things for yourself and hope that some of that will be applicable to others' lives," says one of my clients, the award-winning artist, film director, and teacher Michael Somoroff. "The second way, which is my way, is to search others' needs and create projects that are solutions to their desires. This ensures a certain kind of success because the projects have a place in the world, since people already want them." Somoroff's advice stems from the successes of his own kaleidoscopic career: he's a sought-after lecturer on art and spirituality, his works are at the Museum of Modern Art in New York, and together with Barnett Newman, he is the only artist who was invited to install a work at the renowned Rothko Chapel in Houston. He's also one of the most successful commercial film directors in the world.

▪ **Become an insider.** You don't have to be a braggart to promote yourself effectively. "In my experiences in both TV news and acting, two very competitive fields, it's not only the bold self-promoter who gets ahead," says actor and longtime TV anchor Brad Holbrook. "At first, those people who are more reluctant to draw attention to themselves often end up in roles that are less 'glamorous,' like being a writer or producer in TV news. But once you're inside the realm, a lot of the imagined intimidation can fall away. So that if you're really interested in taking on a more 'out there' job—reporter or actor, say—it might not seem so unimaginable."

■ **Get other people to spread your ideas.** "Self-promotion is a misnomer," says marketing guru and internationally bestselling author Seth Godin. "We've entered an era in which what you really want is 'other-people promotion.' The people who have the most impact aren't the ones who are promoting themselves. They're the ones that other people are promoting. Chuck Close is a famous artist who doesn't jump up and down on the stage—he's in a wheelchair. People talk about him and his work is promoted heavily." Godin adds: "But not by Chuck Close. So the opportunity is to not use your introversion as an excuse. It's to say: 'If I really did remarkable work that changed the status quo in a scary big way, people would talk about me.' And that is your obligation."

Now that we've talked about how to promote yourself to Jo(e) Extrovert, you may wonder how to apply these tips when you promote yourself to an introvert. That may be more instinctual for you; after all, you probably have more needs and pet peeves in common with other introverts. So it should come as no surprise that tips like "show your expertise" are more likely to be well received by an introvert than "interrupt."

Of course, I don't mean to suggest that you are just like all other introverts or that you'll understand their cultural sensitivities, politics, religious beliefs, enthusiasms, insecurities, or personal sense of style. However, you may have certain preferences in common, such as thinking before you speak, which would make it easier for you to communicate with each other. The tricky part is that you can never really be sure who is an extrovert and who is an introvert—especially among more polished, senior-level types—unless they tell you. However, just being attuned to the differences between introverts and extroverts and paying attention to your conversation partner's cues will give you a jumpstart.

PUT YOURSELF OUT THERE

As I mentioned earlier, while I was writing this book, I encountered an array of celebrities. Since they are masters at visibility, I sought advice from them—regardless of where they were on the introversion-extroversion spectrum—to share with you. Of course, there's been much speculation about which public figures are introverts. However, as we've discussed, it can be hard to be sure. Some are introverts who are outgoing in the public eye. Others may be extroverts who are camera-shy about their private lives. I've found that many people either don't know or don't readily disclose whether they're actually introverts, especially in light of the stigma around introversion. Regardless of all that, each time I spotted one of these celebrities, it would have been much easier to do nothing. However, that's exactly what the easy way would have gotten us: nothing. So each time it felt right, I strategized, steeled myself, rehearsed in my head, and approached each of them.

Of course, as a New Yorker, I've seen many celebrities over the years. I've never wanted to invade their quiet time, risk rejection, or, worse, make a scene. This is my introvert's reticence, anyhow. Maybe it's my dread of being perceived as a lunatic fan (Message to negative self-talk: "Shhh ... !"). Before writing this book, I had never approached a celebrity. Now that I've done so, it occurs to me that I probably fade into the big blur of fans who approach these icons all the time. And moments later, in their minds I probably morph into a blonde with curly hair. It helps to think so anyway.

During these encounters, I briefly told the celebrities I spoke with about this book, and I asked what advice they would give my introverted readers. In some cases, they agreed to comment, but not on the spot. Many e-mails, phone calls, faxes, and months later, I learned that "my people following up with their people" was not a productive strategy. A better use of my time was to get a quote, then and there. After all, I needed to spend most of my time writing rather than breaking down the doors of celebrities' gatekeepers.

My judgment (or eyesight) isn't always perfect. On one occasion, I'm out with Isaac at a restaurant in Midtown Manhattan when I notice a guy with a goatee who looks like Craig Newmark, founder of the groundbreaking and ubiquitous craigslist. He arrives with a large group of mostly geeky looking guys and a couple of women. Newmark happens to be high on the list of people I want to interview for this book. The only problem is that I'm not sure if this particular goateed guy is actually THE Craig. So Isaac opens his laptop and we search for him on Google Images. By the time we can pull a photo, Goatee Guy and his party are off to a different room, so I ask Isaac to go check him out. Isaac comes back and says it could be Craig but the guy in question looks maybe a little younger. An hour later, Goatee Guy and his friends exit the restaurant—and I launch. I trail them until they stop in front of the building, and then I tap Goatee Guy on the shoulder. "Are you Craig of craigslist?" I ask. He says, "No," makes a face, and I'm back in high school. I apologize, slink away, and run back to Isaac.

Coincidentally, I discover that the real Craig Newmark is coming to town to speak at NYU in a few weeks. Perfect: NYU, home turf. He and other entrepreneurs who were interviewed in David Vinjamuri's book *Accidental Branding* are scheduled to speak at the book's launch event. So when the day comes, Newmark speaks eloquently and authentically. Then he leaves the auditorium, but it's clear he'll stick around for the book signing. I slip out to see if I can spot him. He's talking to someone, maybe a journalist. I stand there in a neutral stance, not too close, but not too distant. At least I know it's the real Craig this time!

As he finishes his conversation, Newmark turns to me. We say hello, shake hands, and I tell him what I'm up to. He's sure-footed, his eye contact is steady, he speaks clearly and directly, and he relates to the introverts' experience. When I ask him what advice he would give my introverted readers to help them raise their visibility, he says: "Do some good reading, and then talk to people about it. Some of the books by Deborah Tannen, particularly *You Just Don't Understand: Women and Men in Conversation*, are very good." He offers some practical advice: "The next step might be to use some social networking mechanisms, which connect you to people but are a little bit removed and have more of a comfort level. For instance, you might do some blogging or get involved in whatever social networking site fits you personally. It could be Facebook, MySpace, or something else—it's very individual. And then connect in real life with the people you meet online."

INTERVIEWING A MEDIA MOGUL

True to my introverted nature, I spend several hours preparing for a 20-minute phone interview with Cathie Black. I read her book *Basic Black* and scour Hearst.com and every relevant article and audio and video clip I can find. Finally, I go to my local bookstore and pile my arms high with Hearst magazines, from *Cosmopolitan* to *Esquire*, figuring that there's a piece of Black in the look and feel of all of these magazines.

Cathie Black runs a tight ship. Her assistant, Pamela Murphy, keeps me posted when Black is running just a few minutes late. I ask Murphy if her boss would prefer if I address her as "Ms. Black" or "Cathie." She says "Ms. Black" would be fine initially; however, Black would probably invite me to call her Cathie. Got it.

The phone rings. I take a deep breath, do a quick sound check to ensure there are no cotton balls in my voice, and then I answer in a big, clear voice: "Good afternoon. This is Nancy Ancowitz." "Hi, this is Cathie Black." I respond, "Hi, Cathie," as if the doctor has just tapped the reflex spot on my knee. Oy! "Er, Ms. Black," I correct myself, watching that my pitch stays in its natural place rather than an octave higher. What is one of the 50 most powerful women in the world doing calling me directly? Come to think of it, she says in her book that she makes her own calls. I have to quickly recoup, stay grounded, and move on with the call. We do. I had e-mailed her my questions in advance. She answers all of them graciously and eloquently. So nothing really bad happens. Had I made a big deal about my slipup, I think it would have been a much bigger deal than it actually turns out to be.

Why am I telling you about this? Because even with the best preparation, things often don't go as planned, so we need to be flexible, expect a few surprises—from ourselves, others, and our circumstances—and project confidence, no matter what happens.

ASKING THE RICHEST MAN ALIVE A QUESTION

I have to tell you about my magic moment with the Oracle of Omaha, Warren Buffett. Isaac and I went to the Berkshire Hathaway Inc. annual meeting, where Chairman Buffett and his business partner, Charlie Munger, hold court, luminously answering every question under their shareholders' sun during a five-hour Q&A. We had attended this highly informative and entertaining public forum the year before, and we couldn't wait to return—this time with a special agenda.

The night before the annual meeting, at a dinner gathering of the Motley Fool investors' group that Isaac belongs to, he and I sleuthed around for the inside scoop: How could we be among the lucky 50 or so question askers out of the more than 30,000 attendees? We knew that Buffett and Munger answered questions on a first-come, first-served basis, but how on earth would we get a good place in line? Note to introverts: It's much easier to work a room when you have a specific mission. Several of the people we asked—introverts, no doubt—replied that they had never felt they had any questions that were significant enough to pose to Buffett.

While we couldn't find anyone who had actually asked Buffett a question, Isaac's buddy, Mike Klein, Ph.D., gave us a hot tip: Line up in the overflow room, where the meeting would be broadcast live on oversized video screens. Of course, the rest of the crowd would get to see Buffett and Munger live.

Early on the morning of the annual meeting, the doors to the massive Qwest Center in Omaha open, and a line that could lasso the perimeter of Nebraska funnels in. Blast off! I imagine Pamplona during the running of the bulls. Isaac and I chase Klein's rumor up escalators, around amphitheater passageways, and down blind alleys until we enter our own personal Oz—the massive, still-empty overflow room.

Two congenial officials greet us and put our names on the Q&A sign-up sheet. We're first and second in line at Station 13. (Thank you, Mike Klein!) Isaac graciously lets me go first, which means that I'll wait for the first person in each of the other 12 stations to ask Buffett a question before it's my turn. Once we sign up, Isaac and I are free to find a quiet spot to rehearse. I take a few deep breaths and practice my delivery and Isaac reminds me not to rush.

We return to the overflow room during question 10, and I stand at the mike until it's my turn. I practice silently, mouthing the words, as if I were about to sing the national anthem at the World Series. "Question number 13," bellows Buffett from the mammoth video screens, over the heads of thousands of people to my left and right, who are now filling the overflow room. After saying my name and where I'm from, I give my NYU affiliation and say that I'm writing this book for introverts. Then I croon into the microphone: "What advice would you give to the quieter half of the population to help them raise their visibility in their careers?"

I'm prepared for anything, up to and including being summarily expelled from the arena for asking an irrelevant question. Except I never could have anticipated what actually happens: One of the world's richest men, and one of its best off-the-cuff speakers, tells me that he used to be terrified of public speaking and that I am doing something very worthwhile in teaching that skill! (For his advice to you, see Chapter 6.) Luckily, I'm not required to respond because about all I could have managed would have been a *Honeymooners*-style "homina, homina, homina." Then, to top things off, Munger chimes in with one of the zingers he's famous for: "It's a pleasure to have an educator come here who's doing something simple and important instead of foolish and unimportant." Isaac and I celebrate the answers and then quickly step out of the overflow room to rehearse his question, which is in the second round. Later, when we visit Klein and his wife in the Motley Fool section of the arena, we're congratulated as if we had just won the lottery.

BLING STRUCK

Late one weekend night, as Isaac and I are walking toward my home, we notice a big entourage of young, athletic looking black men and a large guy wearing a high-wattage, star-spangled, bling-studded jacket crossing the street toward a spotless, black, armored-looking Escalade SUV. Isaac and I love bling, and we were even wearing some under our coats. I ask an onlooker who the man in the dazzling jacket is. The onlooker, who is missing two front teeth and holding up a lamppost, confirms that it's Don King—just as Isaac has suspected. Isaac and I have a rapid-fire couple's conference in shorthand talk: "I love the jacket. We have to talk to him. Maybe a quote? He's an amazing poet-orator. Ohmigod, we have to try. Okay? Let's go." We approach him hands free. No purse, no cell phone, nothing weaponlike. Common sense.

We're lugging our laptops, so we jog them over to my doorman, and I remove only my palm-sized, bling-studded digital audio device from my purse. We catwalk across the street to the SUV. I rap lightly on the darkened window on the front passenger side. A very Russian Russian rolls down the window and says something to the effect of, "What do you want?" In one breathless sentence, I mutter some jumble of: "NYU," "PROFESSOR," "McGRAW-HILL," "THE JACKET IS A KNOCKOUT," and "QUOTE," while smiling maybe too anxiously for a convincing Duchenne.

The Russian Russian asks me for my full name and phone number, which he punches into his phone. He tells me I can speak with King the next day. "You have a message waiting for you."

I ask if we could just say a quick hello to King right then (pretty please). The window behind him rolls down, and King and all of his bling beam back at us. I tell him I love the way his jacket lit up the street and that I want to ask him a question for my book. With the look of a big man who has just eaten a big meal and wants to call it a night, he puts out his hand and we shake. I introduce Isaac. I say, "I love your jacket." He wearily replies, "God bless." "God bless," I say.

I have a quick debate inside my head about whether I should seize the moment by pushing and asking an interview question for my book. Deciding instead to abide by the Russian, Isaac and I head back to my building and check my cell phone. The Russian has already called. I call him back, and he says that King is resting up for a big fight but that I can call his assistant the following day. Which I do. The assistant asks me to fax my request. She says King would consider, yadda yadda yadda. And even though I never got more of a bona fide quote from King than "God bless," I couldn't refrain from trying. After all, as King is known to say: "Only in America." God bless.

BILL CLINTON'S INNIE

I often would go to a certain quiet Park Avenue hotel lounge to work on this book. I won't name the hotel, but it rhymes with Schmo's Decency. One night, as I am approaching a table in the cozy room, a man at the lively table next to mine smiles at me. He looks just like Bill Clinton, only he's better looking. I start fishing in my purse for my noise-canceling earplugs, which help me submerge into my introvert's bubble to write, when the maître d' heroically dives between me and the other table. It is only then that I become aware of two *Terminator 2* types with clear plastic squigglies in their ears sitting at the next table. Apparently, the man who looks like Bill Clinton *is* Bill Clinton. So I take the only remaining table, about 15 feet away.

I have to talk to him. I have to get a quote for my book. I have to be fearless and free of excuses. How can I ask my introverted readers to step out and promote themselves if I, their introverted author, am not willing to do so myself? I think to myself: I'm a private person, and I don't want to invade Clinton's space. Counterthought: He's a public servant sitting in a public place, facing the public—me.

So what's an introvert to do? I run to the restroom and call Isaac. Urgently, giddily, we strategize: I will send our former commander in chief a drink. In retrospect, this isn't the worst idea ever, but it's close. I dash back to the lounge, where I tell the maître d' what I'm up to and ask, "What's he having?" Gently humoring me, the maître d' advises me to talk to the guys with the squigglies.

I take my seat, which is next to the Secret Service guys and facing Clinton, who is making big, extroverted gestures. The waiter asks me, "Will your boyfriend be joining you tonight?" Followed by: "Would you like your usual?" Perfect timing to dispel suspicions that I'm a WMD-toting madwoman stalker.

"Excuse me," I say to the Secret Service guys. I ask if they're working for "him." Affirmative. My table is between them and the magazine rack. I take an issue of *Gotham* magazine, in which I'm profiled as an executive coach, and then I point to my photograph and interview and say, "See, this is me." I'm not trying to brag; I just want to establish my known-quantity-ness. No response. A more senior looking guy joins the table. I try again. This affable ex-Marine, who has one eye fixed on Clinton at all times, congratulates me. I tell him that this is where I always come to work on my book—that is, Clinton is in *my* space. I say that I would love to ask Clinton, the extrovert's extrovert, to share some of his self-promotion know-how with my introverted readers. He thanks me for asking and says that Clinton wants some private time with Chelsea this evening. However, he says I can try to approach Clinton when he gets up after his meal.

Clinton and company are on their entrées, so I have to casually pretend to write for a while. I chat some more with the Secret Service detail. The senior guy says that almost all Secret Service agents are extroverts, except for one of his staff members, whom he's been mentoring. I give the senior guy my card and encourage him to contact me if he ever thinks that I could help by coaching him or his sole introverted employee. Now he has my picture in a magazine, my business card, and no false moves.

It's getting close to show time. In true introvert fashion, I rehearse my opening line in my head. I recall what writer-actor Laurie Graff told me she had said to Clinton when she spotted him at an Upper West Side café: "I miss you as president." I resolve to deliver something based on that line, only much wittier. Clinton and company get up.

"Excuse me, President Clinton," I say, putting out my hand. "I miss you as president." We shake hands, and I try not to focus on where my wit went. I tell him that I'm writing this book, and I make my request: "Since you're the ultimate extrovert, I would love any advice you could give to my introverted readers to help them raise their visibility."

Clinton focuses his intense gaze on me. The walls of the room fade away. "I'm actually a bit of an introvert," he says. Although he looks at me in earnest, my head fills with the same question that anyone who's turned on a TV in the past 20 years would have: Is he being wry, or did he just reveal something shocking? "I need a lot of time alone," he adds, thoughtfully, demonstrating that he actually understands what an introvert is. Everything I thought I knew about the world comes crashing to the floor, but somehow I'm able to hear the rest: "The advice I'd give is to just throw yourself out there, like mud against a wall. Get out there, and make it happen. Just keep at it." We stand frozen for a moment, like very large moths in amber, until Chelsea takes hold of his hand and pulls him away. It's midnight, and she wants her famous dad back.

Time starts to move again. The waiters and other patrons converge on Clinton. Everyone wants to shake his hand. As Clinton's party leaves, the senior Secret Service guy drops his card on my table. The maître d' asks if I got what I wanted. Affirmative. The busboy asks what he said. I tell him. Taking Clinton's advice, I'm keeping at it!

What would you have done in my shoes? Would you have introduced yourself to Clinton or quietly observed him from afar? More importantly, perhaps: What do you need to do to get where you want to go? Whom do you need to reach out to, and how will you do it?

THE ONE THAT GOT AWAY

My original plans for this book did not include talking to celebrities. However, Bill Clinton's crossing my path early on in the writing process got me fired up. Not to mention Buffett. My friends joked with me about who would be next. Why not the Dalai Lama? So when Senia Maymin, publisher and editor in chief of PositivePsychologyNews.com, told me that she and her boyfriend had tickets to hear the Dalai Lama speak, I tried to get a ticket to join them. She and I had a good laugh about what a long shot it was to get the chance to ask the Dalai Lama a question amid the masses at Radio City Music Hall. As it turned out, I couldn't get a ticket, and His Holiness took only four questions anyway. But one of them was Maymin's! While her question was about happiness, rather than self-promotion for introverts, I had to be happy for her. And maybe, through one degree of separation, we've got some connection to the Dalai Lama! Maymin asked what makes him the happiest, and in a word, his response was: People.

What makes you happiest? I'm happiest when I'm helping people. And I can do that only if they know that I have something valuable to offer.

Back to the importance of being visible: As we discussed in this chapter, it takes different tactics to reach people who are wired differently. We talked about various perspectives on self-promotion from Jo(e) Extrovert and some of her or his more introverted colleagues. In the next and final section, the Conclusion, we'll tie together everything we've covered in this book. It will be a bit like a tour of Rome in a day. However, my intention is to provide you with some concluding thoughts and reminders to help you move forward with your own self-promotion efforts. Ready?

REFLECTIONS AND ACTIONS

What You Learned

1. _____

_____

_____

2. _____

_____

_____

3. _____

_____

_____

Action: What will you do?	How You'll Do It: What support or further information will you obtain?	Accountability: Whom will you tell about this action?	Completion Date: By when?

Conclusion

I believe that you're gifted. You can do some things better than the rest of the pack. As an introvert, that could mean that you're a wordsmith, a supersleuth, or a mastermind. You get absorbed by activities that Jo(e) Extrovert considers solitary confinement.

While you probably aren't gifted at *everything*, nobody is. However, if you persistently focus on your deficits rather than your gifts, you become your own jail keeper. If you keep your gifts a secret, ask yourself this: How can others benefit from them? And what are the chances that you'll get the recognition and compensation you deserve?

Introversion isn't a deficiency any more than left-handedness is. Many of us introverts, like lefties, live in a world designed for someone else. It's okay if you want to remain in the shadows—as long as that's your choice. I wrote this book to offer you alternatives. Isn't it time for you to get recognized for your ingenuity and accomplishments so you can advance in your career and make greater contributions to society?

I hope that by reading this book you've come to appreciate yourself more, whether you identify with being an introvert or just relate to some introverted characteristics. As an introvert who is self-promotion savvy, you can attract better career opportunities as well as gain more respect and status. Of course, wherever you are and wherever you want to go with your self-promotion efforts are fine with me. I created this book for you to learn at your own pace, and I'm rooting for you.

I've shared my own natural reticence about promoting myself based on my long-held belief that doing so is unbecoming, not to mention the extra push self-promotion takes for me as an introvert. I'd like to advance the concept of self-promotion in the spirit of sharing. I've encouraged you to engage in self-promotion as a way of connecting with others, building your network, and offering your knowledge—all of which are not bad things, after all.

Self-promotion may work best for you as an introvert when you get to know people over time, and when you welcome them to get to know you. It's from that place that you'll want to help each other and spread the word about your respective talents. The old saw "one hand washes the other" is a crude approximation of this notion; self-promotion doesn't have to be quid pro quo. I enjoy the endless possibilities that come from introducing people in my network. I also benefit by gaining a reputation as a connector. What's more, people in my network look out for me, in turn, and I usually don't have to ask.

So where have we gone together, and where are you going from here? Did you read this book from cover to cover, or did you skip around? Did you pick it up during a free moment here, a free moment there? Regardless, let's take a moment to recap, reflect on, and reinforce what you learned, and then we'll determine where you'd like to go from here. Capture all of your takeaways from this book in the table at the end of this section. Doing so may be a helpful learning tool for you.

In Chapter 1 we went inward, a place where we're most at home as introverts. We looked at the menace of negative self-talk and its close cousin, perfectionism. We established how both can thwart our visibility by choking our self-expression. When we repeatedly scold and berate ourselves, we set the bar so high that it's unreachable. So you identified the nasty messages you say to yourself and came up with refutations. While I'm not suggesting that you lower your standards, why not be kinder to yourself? Doing so will free you up to experiment, stretch, and enjoy your learning process, rather than get stuck. Remember that no one besides you can hear the nasty messages you say to yourself. So the better you manage them, the more confident you'll be at promoting yourself. After tackling a swim in the bubbly stew of your soul-eating self-talk, we identified your key strengths and accomplishments, which are the backbone of your ability to promote yourself confidently.

In Chapter 2 I asked you to embrace what's special and different about you. As an introvert, that may include your gifts at researching, concentrating, attaining expertise, writing, and listening. We not only looked at what inhibits you but also at what brings out your strengths, including the touchstones (e.g., people, places, and things) that ground you. We explored the time-tested practice of reciting daily affirmations to help pump you up and remind you that you're good enough, that you're smart enough, and that, dog-gone it, people like you, to paraphrase Al Franken's memorable character, Stuart Smalley, a vintage *Saturday Night Live* classic. Despite this groundswell of unrelenting positivity, we acknowledged that we all have off days and can be vulnerable to the sinkhole of comparing ourselves unfavorably to others. We talked about the vital importance of being authentic when we promote ourselves. When we come from a place of truth, we're stronger and more vibrant, which makes us more attractive when we promote ourselves. Imagine a continuum of self-promotion possibilities, from being completely authentic on one far side to being self-absorbed and pretentious on the other far side. Where do you need to be? Remember the billboard you designed that summarizes your message to your audience? Consider what it says and looks like as you're launching or further developing your personal brand.

In Chapter 3 we identified the act of planning as one of your introvert's power tools, and we plugged it in. To propel yourself forward, you started by doing what you do best naturally: You went inward and pondered quietly behind the scenes. We looked at what motivates us, and I suggested that you set goals and deadlines to help get you where you want to go. To avoid getting overwhelmed, we broke things down into small, attainable steps. You created a marketing mix, or a combination of self-promotion activities, that best suits you. So if you like to write, in your marketing mix you can include e-mails, blogs, newsletters, and letters to the editor of publications you value. If you like public speaking, you can create podcasts, teleseminars, and adult education classes. We looked at the vast array of ways to promote yourself to help you pick those that play most to your strengths. We also got concrete about managing the moving parts of every self-promotion effort: time, energy, and money. We acknowledged our introvert's need to recharge our energy alone; we also asked ourselves when we'd benefit from bouncing our plans and ideas off others. Everything we did—or planned to do—tied back to your strengths. No fire walking here. While we anticipated stumbling blocks to prevent you from getting derailed, we never lost sight of what you and others gain when you spread your word to more people.

In Chapter 4 we stepped into the shoes of your boss, your prospective clients, and your other partners in the dance of self-promotion. I also asked you to reflect on what it's like when someone else is promoting herself to you. We discussed a number of different approaches your conversation partners might take from talking only about themselves, bragging, name-dropping, or not showing interest in you to using humor appropriately, listening carefully, and connecting. What works swimmingly, and what bombs? "Duh," you say? Okay, *you* might understand what works, yet so many people don't do the obvious.

Being aware of what does and doesn't work when people promote themselves to you is a starting point for figuring out how you can promote yourself—palatably—to your target audience. You turned on that fictional yet popular commercial-only radio station WIIFM, or What's In It For Me, to keep yourself attuned to what really matters—first to you, and then to others. We discovered how you could use your wily introvert's strengths to excel at promoting yourself without doing anything embarrassing or beneath you. In this chapter I reminded you that your target audience isn't "el mundo," which should come as a relief to most introverts. You don't have to knock yourself out trying to appeal to everyone. Instead, just figure out how to deliver value to a very tiny slice of the planet. We looked at what you have to offer as well as what makes you hire someone and why people hire you. We did a lot of looking, thinking, and strategizing to get you ready for the more external actions in the chapters that follow.

In Chapter 5 we carried forward the theme of promoting yourself in the spirit of helping others. Once again we tapped into your introverted strengths. Just because you're not a schmoozer by nature doesn't mean you can't be an outstanding networker. Who said you can't meet one-on-one with the people who you really want to get to know, rather than hold up the wall at numerous, noisy social events? I encouraged you to consider one of my favorite networking tools, informational interviews, which are an effective way to get to know just about anyone. It's important to remember what you bring to the table and how valuable you can be in other people's networks as a source of information, insights, and introductions—or even just as a thoughtful listener. I offered you sample e-mail language to help you reach out to people in your network. If you found yourself wondering, "What network?" at the beginning of Chapter 5, I hope that you aren't still saying that after completing the chapter, which has plenty of tools and tips to help you build lasting professional relationships.

In Chapter 6 we looked at ways to make the often daunting experience of giving presentations easier for you as an introvert. Just think of how you can benefit from public speaking. It allows you to deliver your message once to a lot of people all at the same time—rather than wear yourself down, which is bound to happen if you have to repeat yourself and your message dozens of times at scores of smaller forums! It also positions you as an expert on your subject matter; so people will come to you. Of course, giving a good presentation usually takes preparation and rehearsal. You may also need the right level of support from a coach, mentor, or friend, who will help you practice and will offer feedback.

We looked at three aspects of improving your public speaking, or presentation, skills: how to prepare, how to deliver your message, and what to do in a pinch. As usual, we started from the place of your strengths and advantages as an introvert. We also acknowledged where public speaking gets hard for you. Of course, our discussion wouldn't be complete without arming you with tools to help you prevent and manage your jitters. I was right there with you before, during, and after your presentations—all the while offering suggestions to help you enjoy public speaking, which is an excellent way to raise your visibility.

Building on the networking and presentation skills you learned in the prior two chapters, you learned how you can stand out—in a good way—as a candidate on a job interview in Chapter 7. After all, most interviews are one-on-one meetings, which play to our natural strengths as introverts. A hard part of interviewing for us is being put on the spot, which often means having to speak before we have sufficient time to think. So we prepared ourselves to walk into the interview process confidently and ready to handle any question that comes our way. We were reminded that our answers are often less important than how we deliver them. Once again, we found that it pays to be authentic and enthusiastic, to listen carefully, and to practice describing the contributions we can make to prospective employers. We covered how to get ready for your interviews, what to bring, and even what to wear. We talked about the importance of polishing your nonverbal communication skills, anticipating the toughest questions, and readying yourself for salary negotiations. Of course, it doesn't end there. Part of the game is in how well you follow up. While interviewing is a huge topic, we focused mainly on the practical aspects that will help you, as an introvert, get the job.

The most fun—and terrifying (for me, anyhow!)—part about Chapter 8 was my encounters with celebrities. The process of writing this book got me to take more risks than I normally do—and I often lived to tell you the stories. I sometimes wonder whether I was out of my mind for rapping on the darkened window of the billionaire boxing impresario Don King's armored SUV, approaching a heavily guarded President Bill Clinton at a hotel bar, and asking Warren Buffett a question that had nothing to do with investing in front of a crowd of more than 30,000 shareholders at the Berkshire Hathaway annual meeting. I felt a sense of responsibility to you when I approached these masters of visibility. After all, I either had to set an example or fess up about my missteps on these pages.

So I risked morbid embarrassment and, worse, seeing my adventures turn up on YouTube. I asked an array of high-profile people for their advice for you, and they generously obliged. Each of these interactions was a wild ride for me as an introvert. After all, a big part of me would rather stay home and read a book. Instead, I had to write one. So in this chapter I shared the viewpoints of some renowned extroverts as well as those of some high-profile introverts, all of whom have impacted the lives of countless people. They engage in many of the same activities that you and I do to promote ourselves, only on a larger scale, gaining them recognition in spades. And I bet you that they weren't all born to sell.

WHY HIRE A COACH

Reach as high as you'd like to go. If 15 minutes of fame is what you want, then go for it. If you need to be highly visible to make a difference, now you have more tools to do so. If you're aiming to land your dream job, or even if you could just use a stepping-stone to take you closer to that goal, I wish you the courage and fortitude you need to get there. The good news is that you don't have to do it alone—unless you want to.

Remember the dream team you created in Chapter 1? Get the support you need. Hiring an executive coach had a profound impact on my career. It was the key to figuring out my life after Wall Street. There are all kinds of coaching specialties—personal and life, financial planning, career, leadership, health and fitness, and my specialty, which is business communication, just to name a few.

Plenty of studies point to the efficacy of coaching as well as the return on investment it provides. In fact, an article in the *International Coaching Psychology Review* says: "In all the studies undertaken, investigating whatever mode of coaching, the conclusion was the same—everyone likes to be coached and perceives that it impacts positively upon their effectiveness."[1]

You can work with a coach to move some aspect of your life forward—anything from mapping out your career to becoming a better manager to improving your personal relationships. From a long list of possibilities, those are just a few examples. With the right support and guidance, whether it's from a coach, mentor, or a confidante, you can progress much more quickly, easily, and joyfully.

As a business communication coach, my role is that of a thinking partner and stalwart supporter for clients interested in advancing their careers by enhancing their spoken and written communication skills. This could mean building their professional networks, rehearsing their presentations, preparing for their job interviews, strategizing to help them get promotions, and crafting language for their various pitches. Our work together can include brainstorming, role-playing, and creating concrete plans.

Coaching sessions can last anywhere from several minutes to, more typically, an hour or two, and they can be spread out over the course of weeks, months, or even years. In some cases, clients can see results in just one session; however, deeper or more significant changes usually occur over the course of a few months.

How do you find a coach? You can seek word-of-mouth referrals, take a class or a teleseminar with a coach you're interested in, or research coaches on the Web site of the International Coach Federation (ICF), which is the largest worldwide resource for professional coaches. Many coaches offer complimentary introductory sessions. If you think you might benefit from hiring a coach, I strongly recommend speaking with several and going with the one who really "gets" you, hears your concerns, and helps you think more clearly about whatever it is that you want to focus on—not to mention the one who inspires you to make positive changes in your career and life.

Disclaimer: If you suffer from severe depression, debilitating anxiety, substance abuse, domestic violence, or self-destructive behavior, a coach is not qualified to help you. Instead, seek the services of a licensed therapist or other professional trained to help you manage these types of issues. If you're unsure which type of professional is best suited to your individualized needs, check the ICF Web site (www.coachfederation.org), which describes the distinctions between coaching, therapy, consulting, mentoring, training, and even athletic development.

While the world is made up of introverts and extroverts, those are only two measures of describing a complex human being. No matter where you fall on the spectrum, I urge you to share your knowledge and other gifts; I also urge you to get the credit you deserve for your accomplishments. When? Why not now? It's a fine time to celebrate yourself and all the good you can bring the world. So once more, inward, outward, and onward—and I hope you enjoy the journey!

REFLECTIONS AND ACTIONS—SUMMARY

Write your three biggest takeaways or insights from the entire book in the space that follows.

1. _____

_____

2. _____

_____

3. _____

_____

In the grid that follows take stock of everything you've learned throughout this book, and determine what additional measures you'll take to further your self-promotion efforts. If you've completed the Reflections and Actions section at the end of each chapter, turn back to what you wrote to help you complete this summary. After you've completed the grid, consider consolidating all of your next steps onto a master plan or calendar or entering them into your PDA. To increase your chances of success, let someone you trust in on your plans.

Chapter	What You've Learned	How You'll Apply the Learning	When You'll Apply the Learning
Introduction			
1. Your Negative Self-Talk: Tuning Out U-SUCK Radio			
2. Your Strengths: Tuning In U-ROCK Radio			
3. Your Game Plan: Creating a Winning Marketing Mix			
4. Your Target Audiences: Going Inward and Reaching Outward			
5. Your Network: Expanding Your Sphere of Influence			
6. Your Chalk Talk: Public Speaking for Private People			
7. Your Job Search: Interviewing for Introverts			
8. Your Opposite: The World According to Jo(e) Extrovert			
Conclusion			

Endnotes

Introduction

1. Isabel Briggs Myers, Mary H. McCaulley, Naomi L. Quenk, and Allen L. Hammer, *MBTI Manual: A Guide to the Development and Use of the Myers-Briggs Type Indicator*, 3rd ed., Consulting Psychologists Press, Palo Alto, Calif., 1998, p. 298.
2. Del Jones, "Not All Successful CEOs Are Extroverts," *USA Today*, June 7, 2006, www.usatoday.com/moncy/companies/management/2006-06-06-shy-ceo-usat_x.htm.
3. "Oprah Talks to Jerry Seinfeld," (audio interview), *O, The Oprah Magazine*, November 2007, www.oprah.com/article/omagazine/omag_200711_ocut.
4. Sage Stossel, "Introverts of the World, Unite!" *The Atlantic Magazine*, February 14, 2006, www.theatlantic.com/fs/esearch.php?sort=time&source=magazine&words=rauch&x=0&y=0.
5. Ibid.
6. Elaine Aron, Ph.D., www.hsperson.com, December 1, 2008.
7. Robert Ornstein, *The Roots of the Self: Unraveling the Mystery of Who We Are*, HarperCollins, New York, 1995, p. 55. See also Allen L. Hammer, editor, *MBTI Applications*, chapter written by John Shelton titled "Health, Stress, and Coping," Oxford Psychologists Press, Oxford, United Kingdom, 1996, pp. 198–200.

8. Debra L. Johnson, Ph.D., et al., "Cerebral Blood Flow and Personality: A Positron Emission Tomography Study," *American Journal of Psychiatry*, vol. 156, no. 2, February 1999, pp. 252–257.
9. Daniel Nettle, "The Science Behind Personality," *Independent UK*, September 18, 2007, www.alternet.org/healthwellness/62829/.

Chapter 1

1. A. Gale, "Electroencephalographic Studies of Extraversion-Introversion: A Case Study in the Psychophysiology of Individual Different," *Personality and Individual Differences*, vol. 4., no. 4, 1983, pp. 371–380, cited in Debra L. Johnson, Ph.D., et al., "Cerebral Blood Flow and Personality: A Positron Emission Tomography Study," *American Journal of Psychiatry*, vol. 156, no. 2, February 1999, p. 255.
2. Laura Morgan Roberts, Gretchen Spreitzer, Jane Dutton, Robert Quinn, Emily Heaphy, and Brianna Barker, "How to Play to Your Strengths," *Harvard Business Review*, January 2005.
3. Joann Lublin, "Networking? Here's How to Stand Out," *Wall Street Journal*, November 4, 2008.
4. Lewis Gordon Pugh, "The Ice Bear Cometh, Wearing Nothing but a Speedo," *New York Times*, May 27, 2006, www.nytimes.com/2006/05/27/sports/othersports/27outdoors.html.
5. Michael Winerip, "Phelps's Mother Recalls Helping Her Son Find Gold-Medal Focus," *New York Times*, August 8, 2008, www.nytimes.com/2008/08/10/sports/olympics/10Rparent.html?pagewanted=1.
6. Alice Park, "Big Splash," *Time*, August 14, 2008, www.time.com/time/magazine/article/0,9171,1832873,00.html.

Chapter 2

1. Values in Action (VIA) Signature Strengths Questionnaire, www.authentichappiness.sas.upenn.edu/Default.aspx.
2. Tom Rath, *Strengths Finder 2.0*, Gallus Press, New York, 2007, p. iii.
3. Earvin "Magic" Johnson, *32 Ways to Be a Champion in Business*, Crown Business, New York, 2008, pp. 41, 47.

Chapter 3

1. E. A. Locke and G. P. Latham, "Building a Practically Useful Theory of Goal Setting and Task Motivation: A 35-Year Odyssey," *American Psychologist*, September 2002, p. 706.
2. American Psychological Association (APA) poll conducted by Harris Interactive between April 7 and 15, 2008, "Economy and Money Top Causes of Stress for Americans," apahelpcenter. mediaroom.com/index.php?s=press_releases&item=51.
3. CareerBuilder.com survey conducted by Harris Interactive between May 22 and June 13, 2008, "One in Five Employers Use Social Networking Sites to Research Job Candidates," September 10, 2008, www.reuters.com/article/pressRelease/idUS99235+ 10-Sep-2008+PRN20080910?sp=true.
4. Reid Hoffman, LinkedIn cofounder, interviewed on *The Charlie Rose Show*, March 4, 2009, www.charlierose.com/view/ interview/10128.

Chapter 4

1. Bradford Thomas, Simon Mitchell, and Jeff Del Rossa, *Sales: Strategic Partnership or Necessary Evil? 2007–2008 Global Sales Perceptions Report*, Development Dimensions International, Inc., Bridgeville, Penn., pp. 4, 6.

Chapter 5

1. Gerry Crispin and Mark Mehler, "CareerXroads 2008 Seventh Annual Source of Hire Study: What 2007 Results Mean for Your 2008 Plans," www.careerxroads.com/news/SourcesOfHire08.pdf. CareerXroads is a firm that specializes in the use of technology solutions for meeting business staffing goals.
2. John Tozzi, "The Escalator Pitch," *BusinessWeek*, May 16, 2008, www.businessweek.com/smallbiz/content/may2008/ sb20080516_67308.htm.
3. Randy J. Larsen and Todd K. Shackelford, "Gaze Avoidance: Personality and Social Judgments of People Who Avoid Direct Face-to-Face Contact," *Personality and Individual Differences*, vol. 21, no. 6, Elsevier Science, 1996, pp. 907–917.

Chapter 6

1. "Meditate on This New Finding," *Odyssey*, University of Kentucky, Winter 2007, p. 33.
2. Edward Tufte, "PowerPoint Is Evil: Power Corrupts. PowerPoint Corrupts Absolutely," *Wired.com*, 1993–2004, Condé-Naste Publications; 1994–2003 Wired Digital, Inc., www.wired.com/wired/archive/11.09/ppt2_pr.html.

Chapter 7

1. U.S. Bureau of Labor Statistics, www.bls.gov.
2. Ibid.
3. Jared R. Curhan and Alex Pentland, "Thin Slices of Negotiation: Predicting Outcomes from Conversational Dynamics within the First 5 Minutes," *Journal of Applied Psychology*, vol. 92, no. 3, 2007, p. 802.
4. Alex (Sandy) Pentland, *Honest Signals: How They Shape Our World*, MIT Press, Cambridge, Mass., 2008, pp. 10–12, 31.
5. Society for Human Resource Management (SHRM), 2008 Job Satisfaction Survey, Alexandria, Va., www.shrm.org.
6. Roger Fisher, William Ury, and Bruce Patton, *Getting to Yes: Negotiating Agreement without Giving In*, 2d ed., Houghton Mifflin Harcourt, Boston, 1991, p. 97.

Conclusion

1. Annette Fillery-Travis and David Lane, "Does Coaching Work or Are We Asking the Wrong Question?" *International Coaching Psychology Review*, vol. 1, no. 1, April 2006, p. 35, www.reframe.dk/Does_coaching_work.pdf.

Index

About the Author

A business communication coach specializing in career advancement and presentation skills, Nancy Ancowitz is a thinking partner and stalwart supporter for her clients, who range from CEOs to emerging leaders in the business and creative worlds. She is a mirror who reflects her clients' best selves, a sounding board for their deep intelligence, and a navigator to help their quiet stars twinkle.

An outgoing introvert, Ancowitz is an adjunct instructor at New York University, where she teaches Self-Promotion for Introverts®, a workshop that helps people of a quieter nature use their strengths to raise their visibility in their careers. She also teaches public speaking and other business communication skills. Ancowitz has spoken at the Smithsonian Institution and a wide range of corporate and professional organizations.

Her background includes 12 years in the corporate world, where most recently Ancowitz headed marketing teams for a multi-billion-dollar business as a vice president at JPMorgan Chase & Co. Earlier in her career she was a jewelry designer with major retail clients.

Ancowitz's media exposure as a coach includes CareerJournal. com (the executive career site of the *Wall Street Journal*), CNN.com, Monster.com, the *New York Times*, *Newsday*, WABC-TV *Eyewitness News*, and *Self*, *Woman's Day*, and *Gotham* magazines. Ancowitz's creative expressions include her after-hours life as a playwright. Visit her Web site at www.selfpromotionforintroverts.com.